Animal Camo

GO BOLD OR BE SAFE!

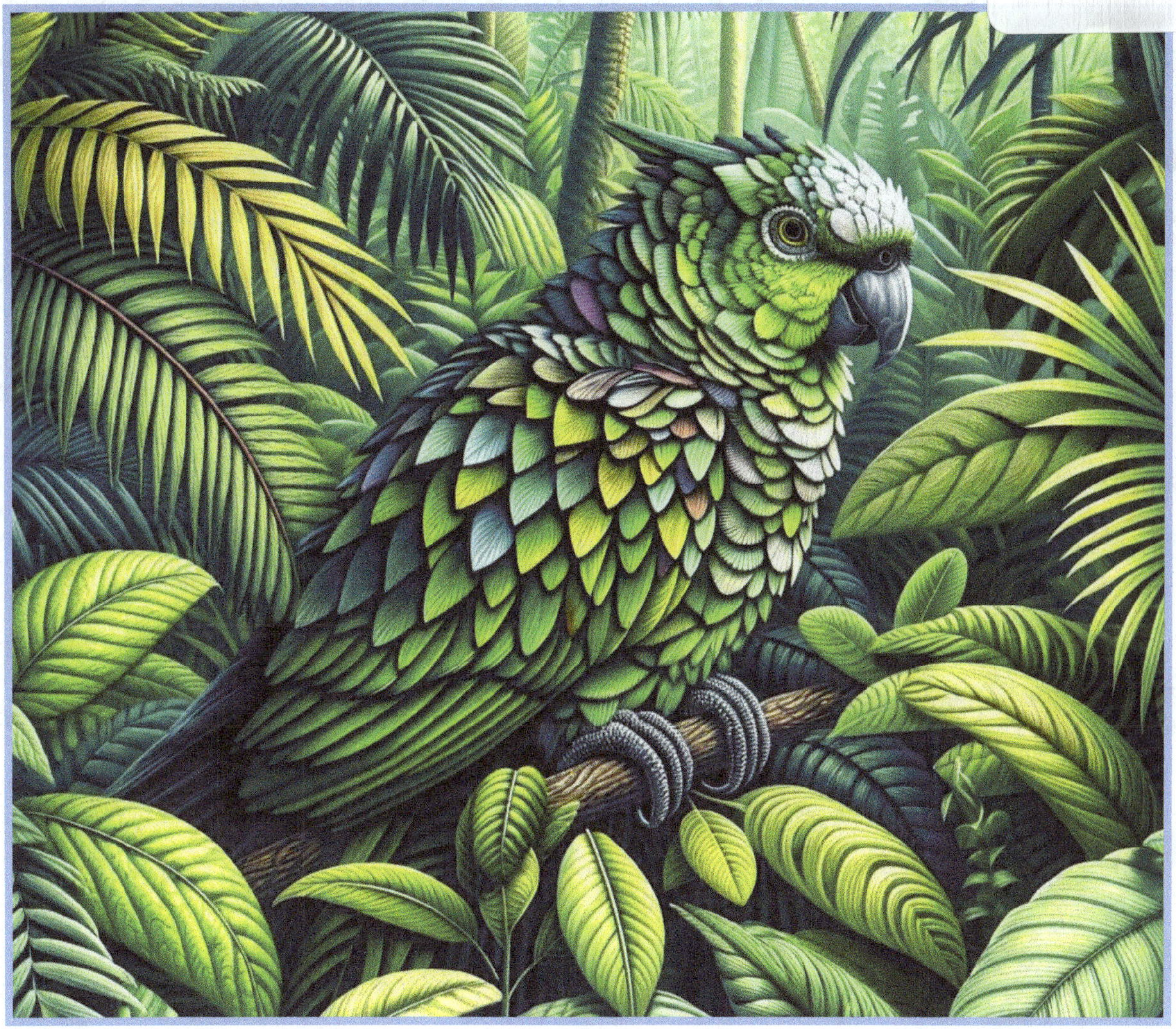

Go Bold or Be Safe!

Get ready for an exciting coloring adventure where nature's greatest masters of disguise take center stage. Within these pages, you'll discover a captivating world of camouflage, where animals blend seamlessly into their surroundings, challenging your perception and creativity.

I have curated a diverse collection of creatures renowned for their remarkable camouflage abilities. From the elusive chameleon to the stealthy snow leopard, each animal represents a unique adaptation to its environment. Prepare to be amazed by the ingenuity of nature as you explore the hidden wonders of the animal kingdom. Each page features a meticulously crafted illustration of the animal's natural habitat, where the line between predator and prey blurs into the landscape.

To enhance your coloring experience, two distinct coloring options are possible for each page. You can unleash your creativity by making the hidden animal stand out with bold and contrasting colors, boldly declaring its presence amid its surroundings. On the other hand, you may want to continue the camouflage palette and seamlessly blend the animal into its environment. The choice is yours - will you go bold or play it safe?

Whether you're a seasoned artist or a budding colorist, this book promises hours of entertainment and discovery. As you immerse yourself in the intricate designs and captivating narratives, you'll gain a deeper appreciation for the wonders of nature and the art of camouflage. Happy coloring!

Jenifer Steller

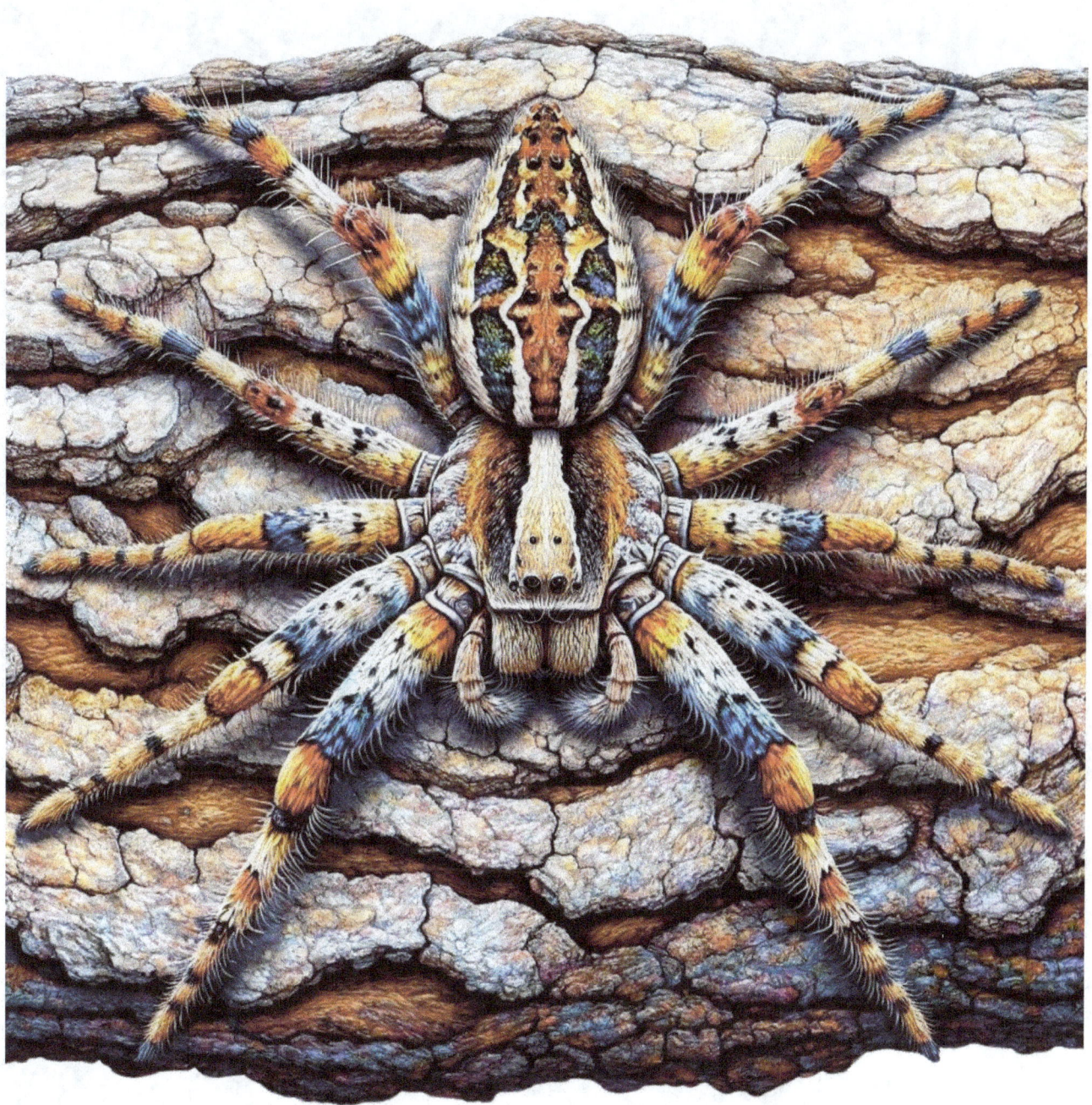

Two-Tailed Spider

Camouflaged on tree bark, the Two-Tailed Spider blends almost imperceptibly with its surroundings, highlighting its unique body structure and the rugged texture of the bark.

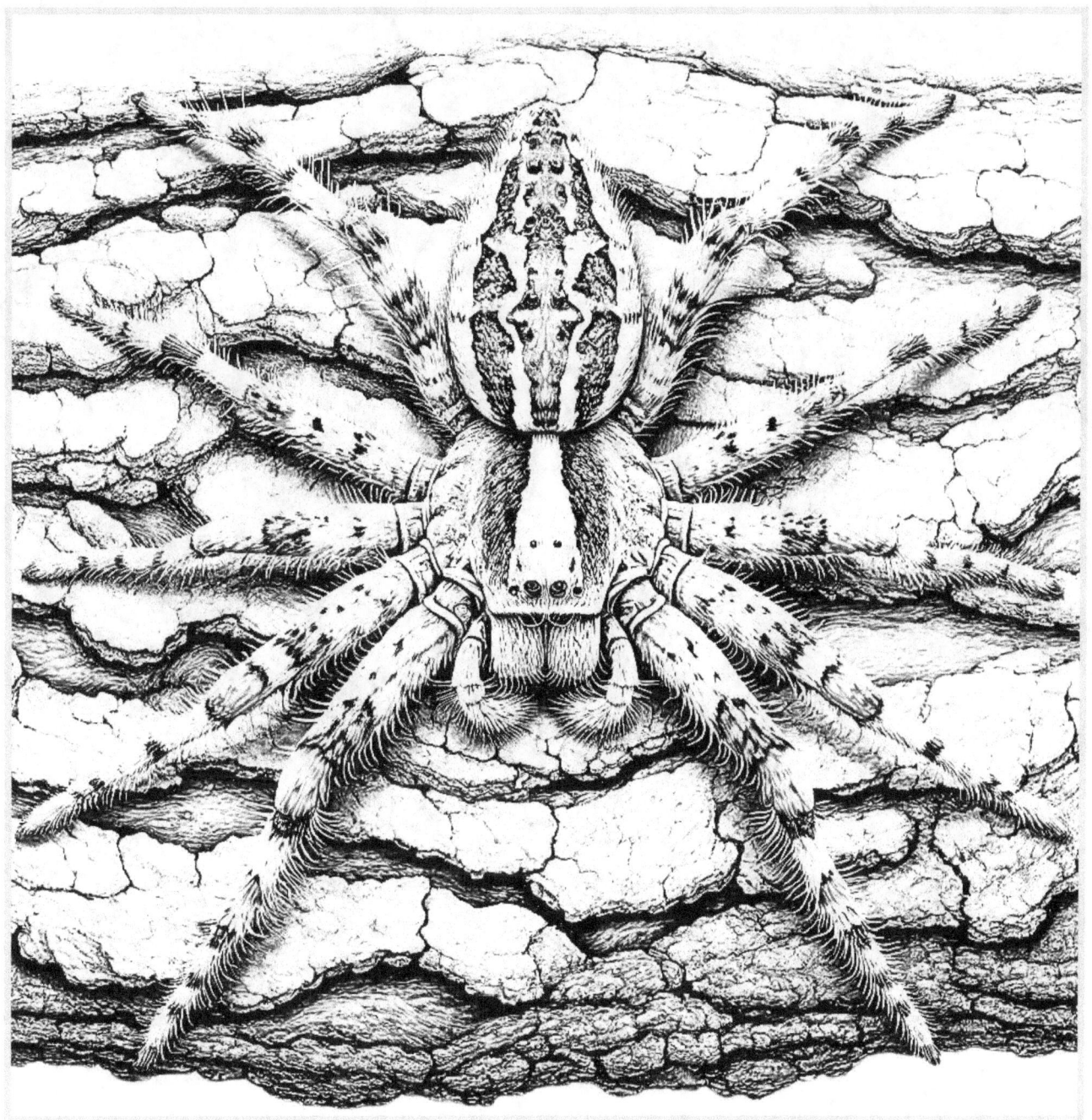

Hobart's Red Glider Butterfly

Hobart's Red Glider Butterfly camouflages itself on a vibrant red flower. This scene captures the butterfly's delicate wing patterns against the lush red petals.

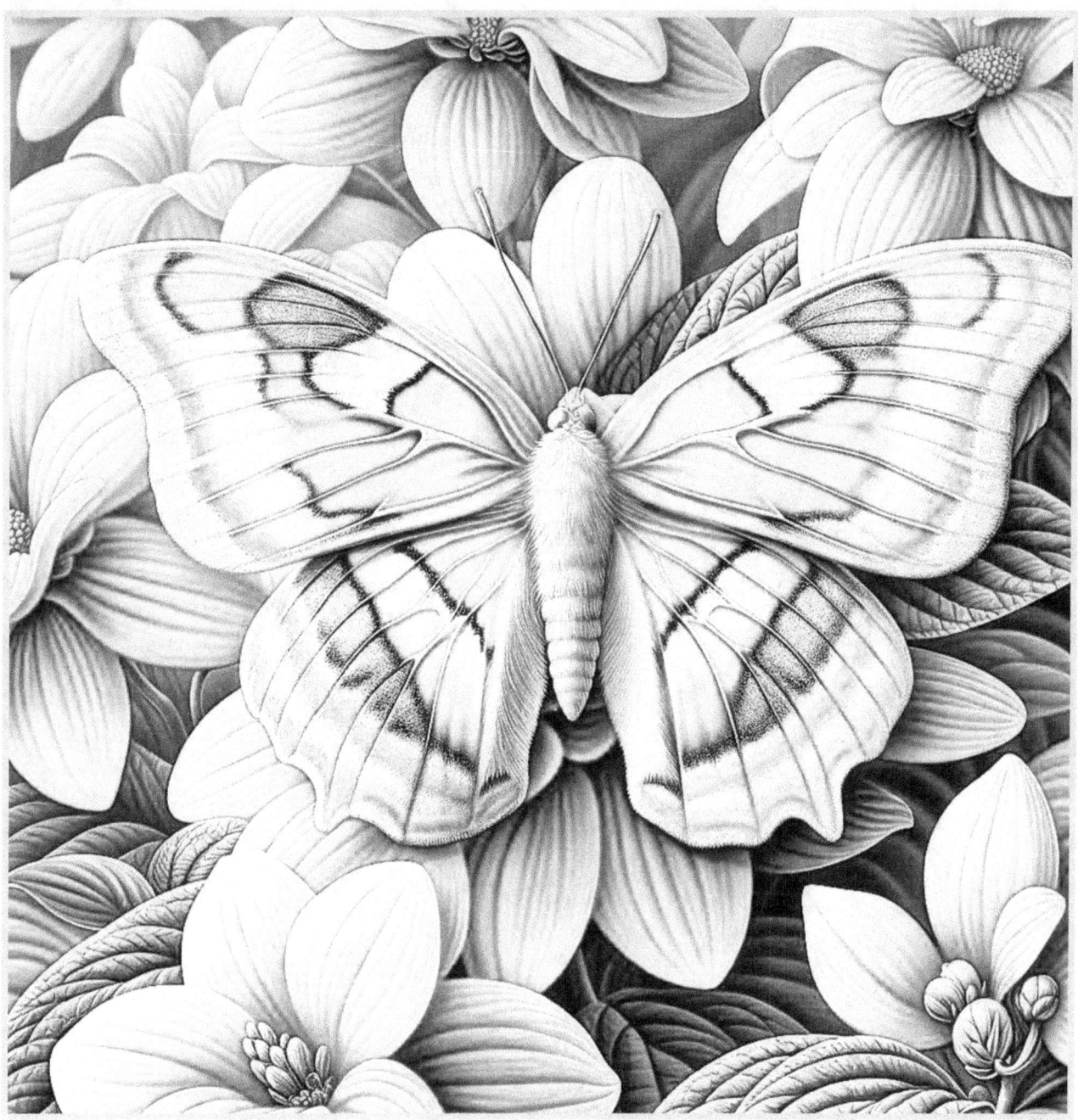

Walking Stick

The Walking Stick seamlessly integrates with twig-like structures, accentuating its long body and limbs that resemble real sticks and branches.

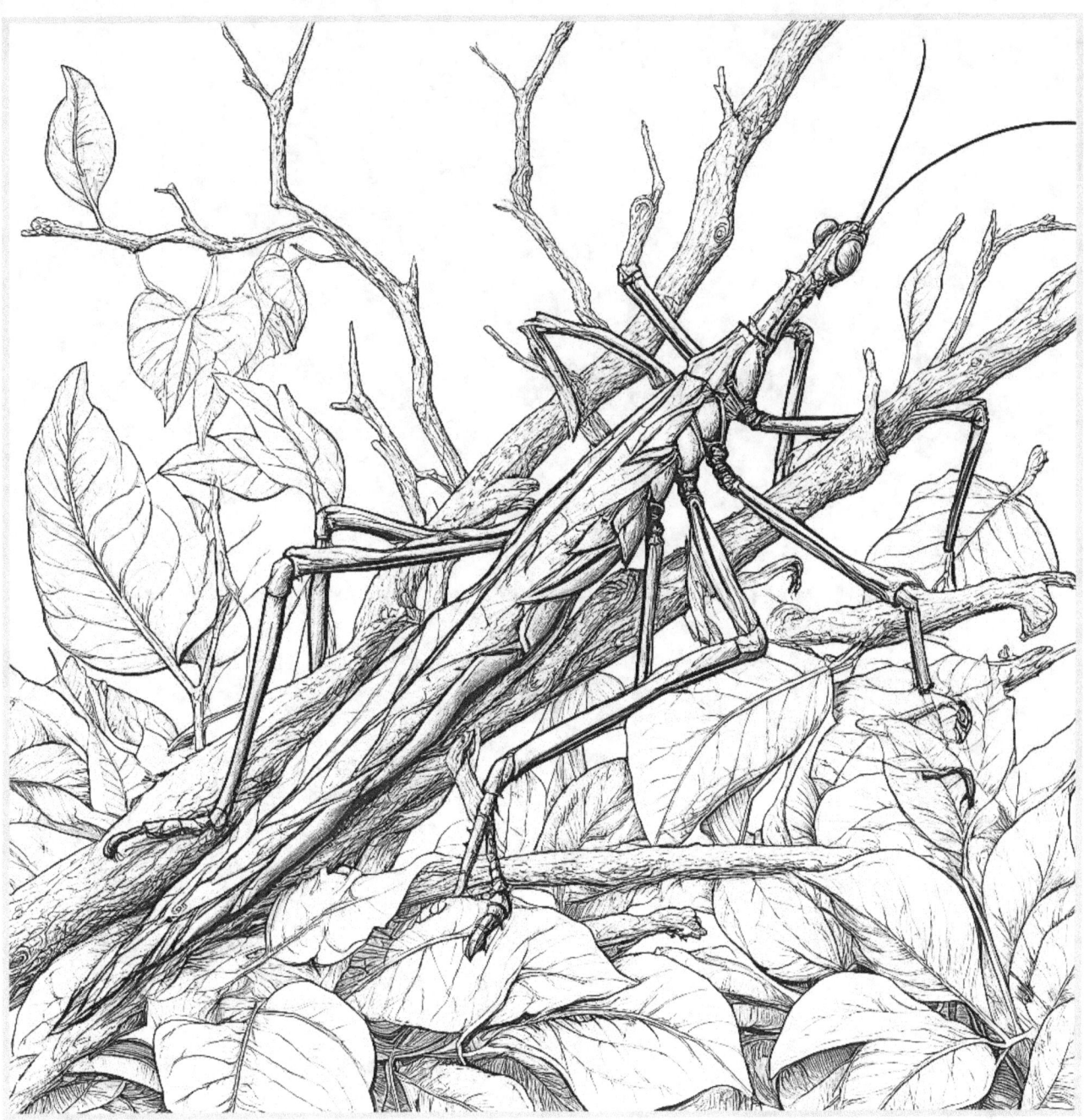

Crab Spider

A crab spider, perfectly blending in with yellow flowers, demonstrates the spider's yellow coloration and the delicate texture of the flowers.

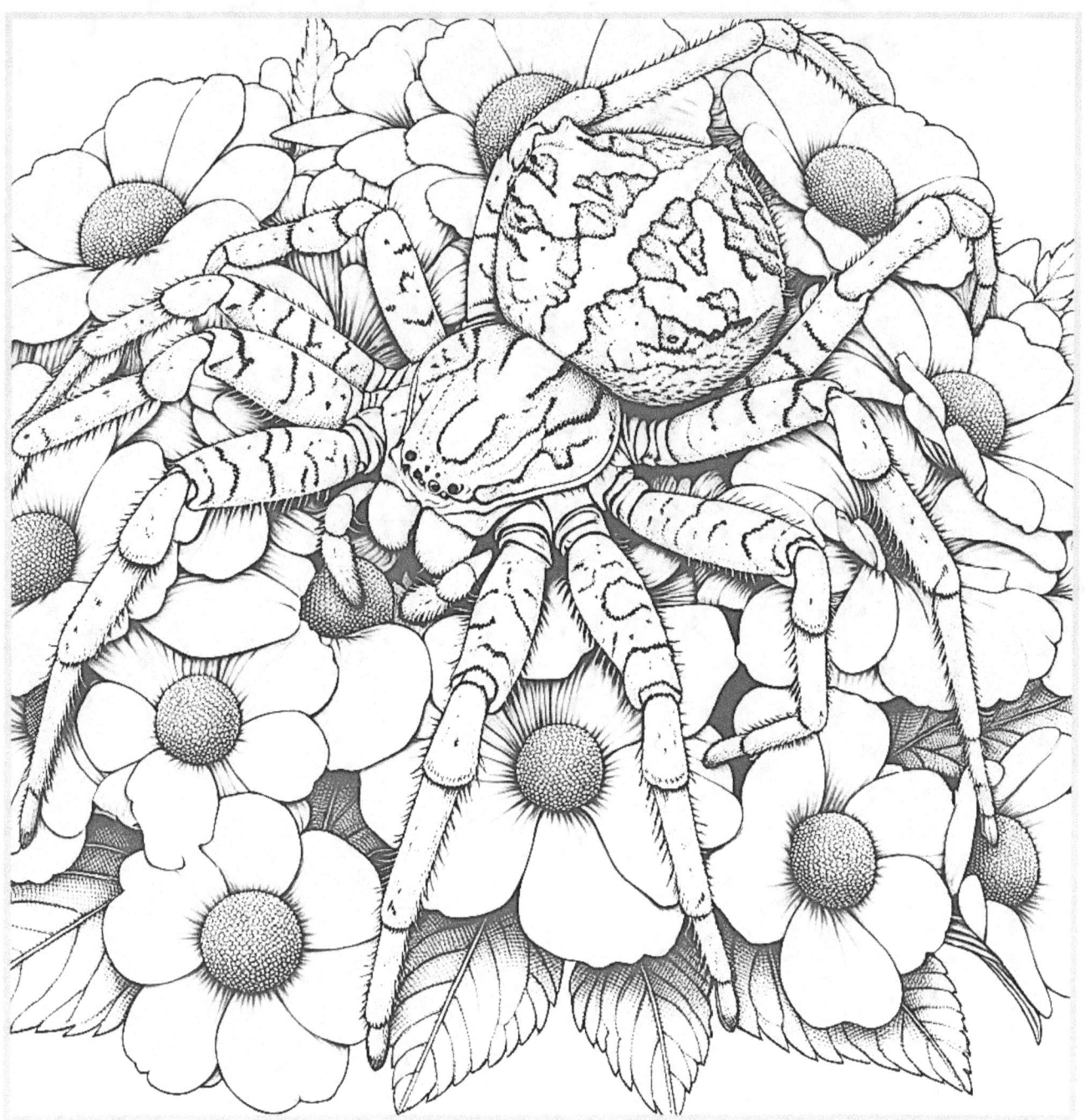

Gray Cracker Butterfly

The Gray Cracker Butterfly blends perfectly with the textured gray tree bark, demonstrating its remarkable camouflage skills. The detailed patterns on its wings mimic the rough texture of the tree bark.

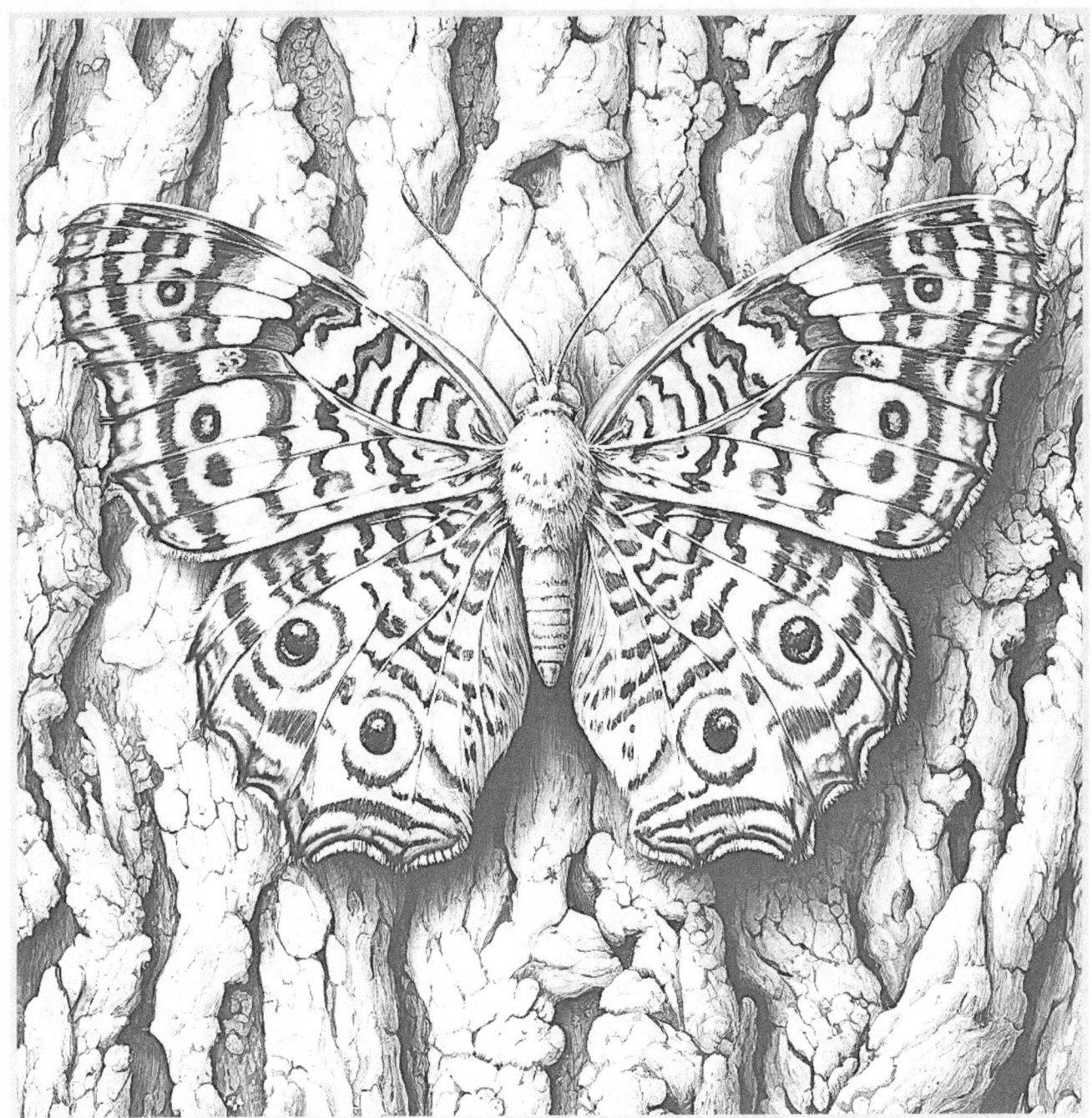

Katydid

Amid the lush green foliage, a Katydid expertly disguises itself, seamlessly merging with the leaf by mimicking its veins and surface texture.

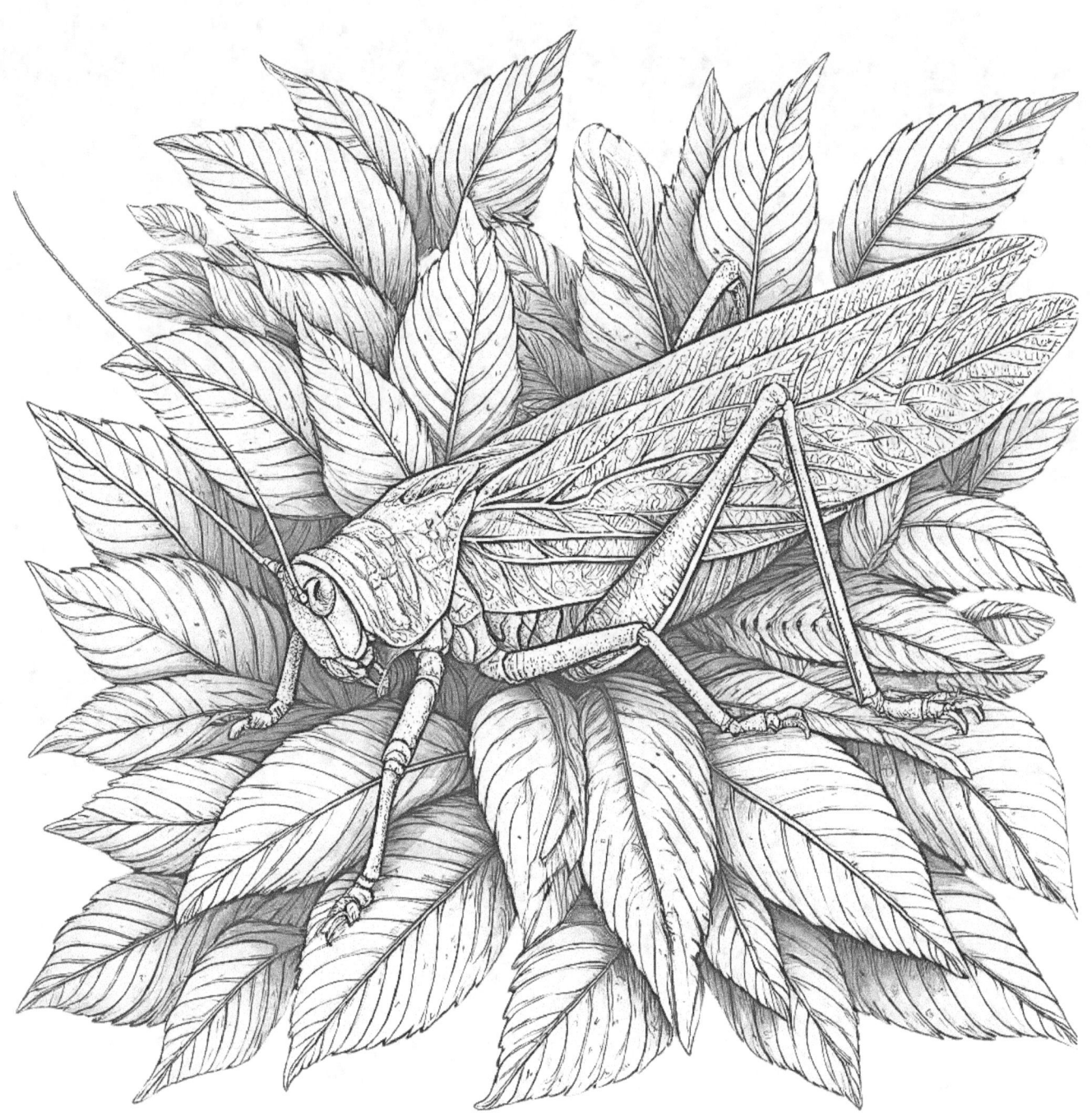

Orchid Mantis

Amid vibrant orchid blossoms, an Orchid Mantis expertly camouflages itself in its environment. This scene captures the mantis effortlessly blending in with the orchid petals, accentuating its delicate stem-like shape with the vivid colors of the flowers.

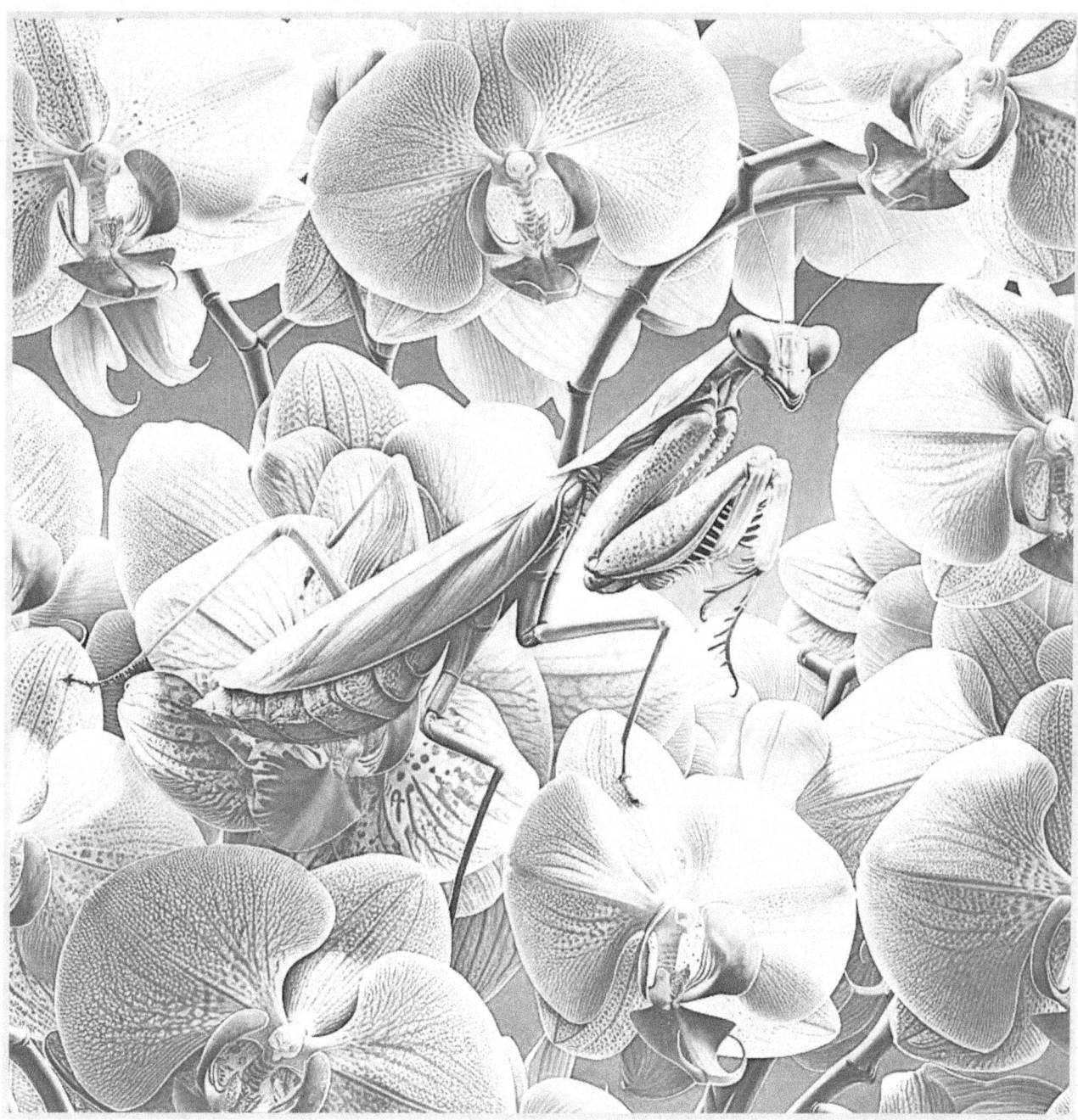

Reed Warbler

The Reed Warbler seamlessly blends into its surroundings, showcasing its brown and beige feathers which perfectly imitate the texture and color of the marsh reeds.

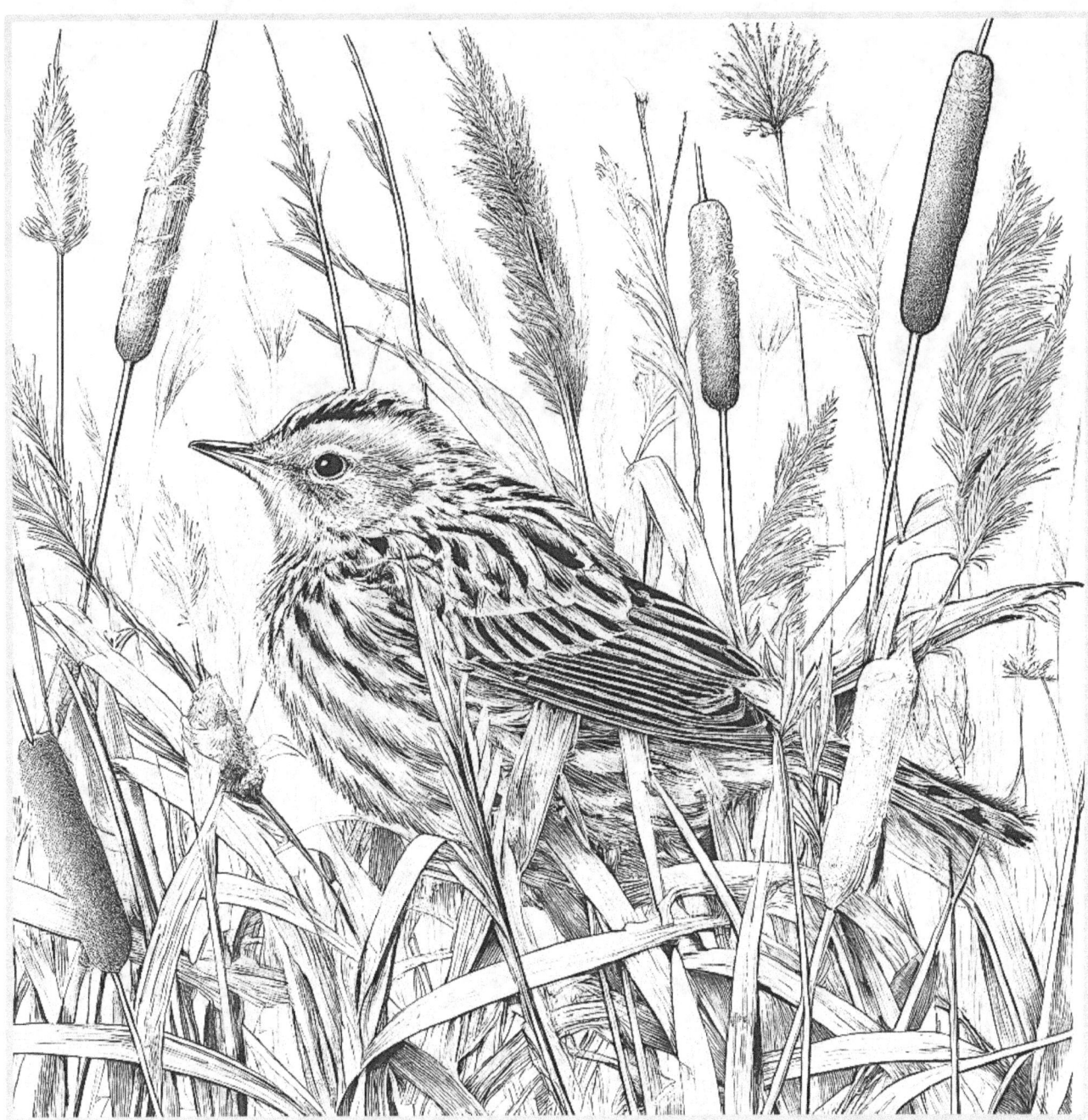

Owl

Among the branches of a tree, an owl perfectly camouflages itself, blending seamlessly with the tree bark. Its feathers mimic the texture and color patterns of the wood, making it almost imperceptible.

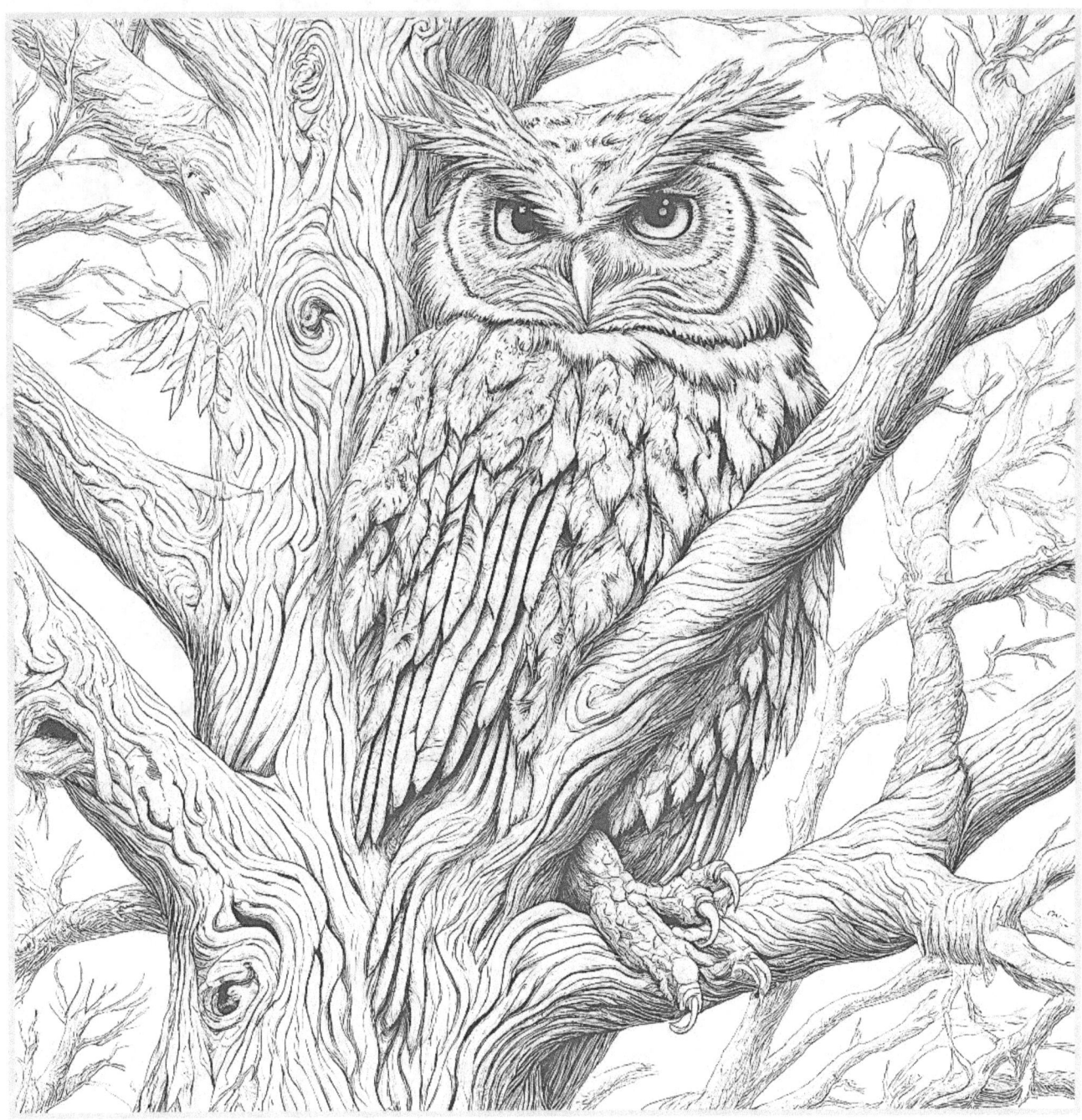

American Bittern

The American Bittern camouflages itself among tall reeds in a marshland setting. This scene captures the Bittern blending with its surroundings, emphasizing its streaked plumage and the dense, textured reeds.

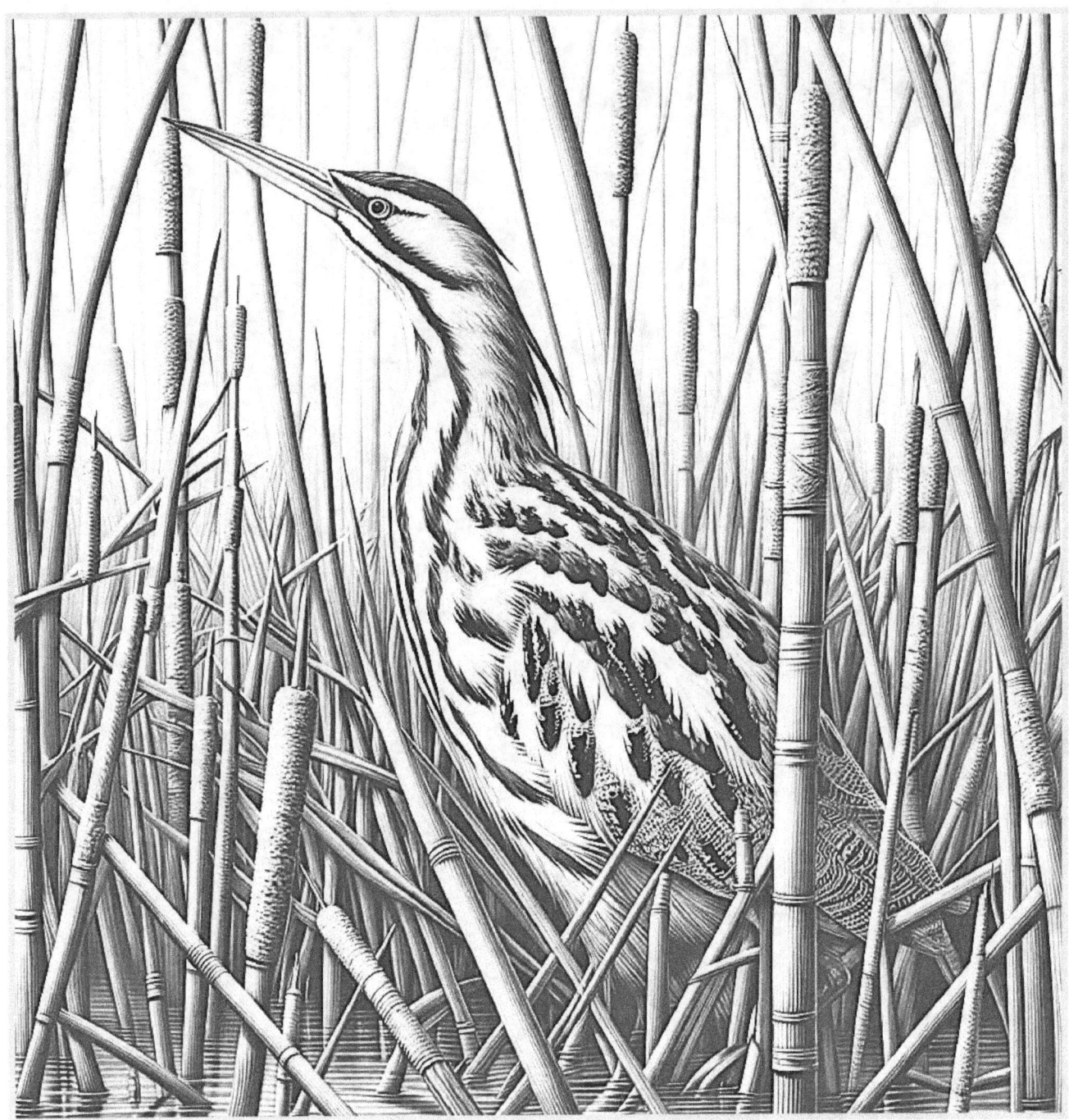

Mealy Amazon Parrot

The Mealy Amazon Parrot seamlessly blends into the vibrant green foliage of a tropical rainforest, almost disappearing in the lush surroundings. Its green plumage complements the dense tropical backdrop, creating a striking natural camouflage.

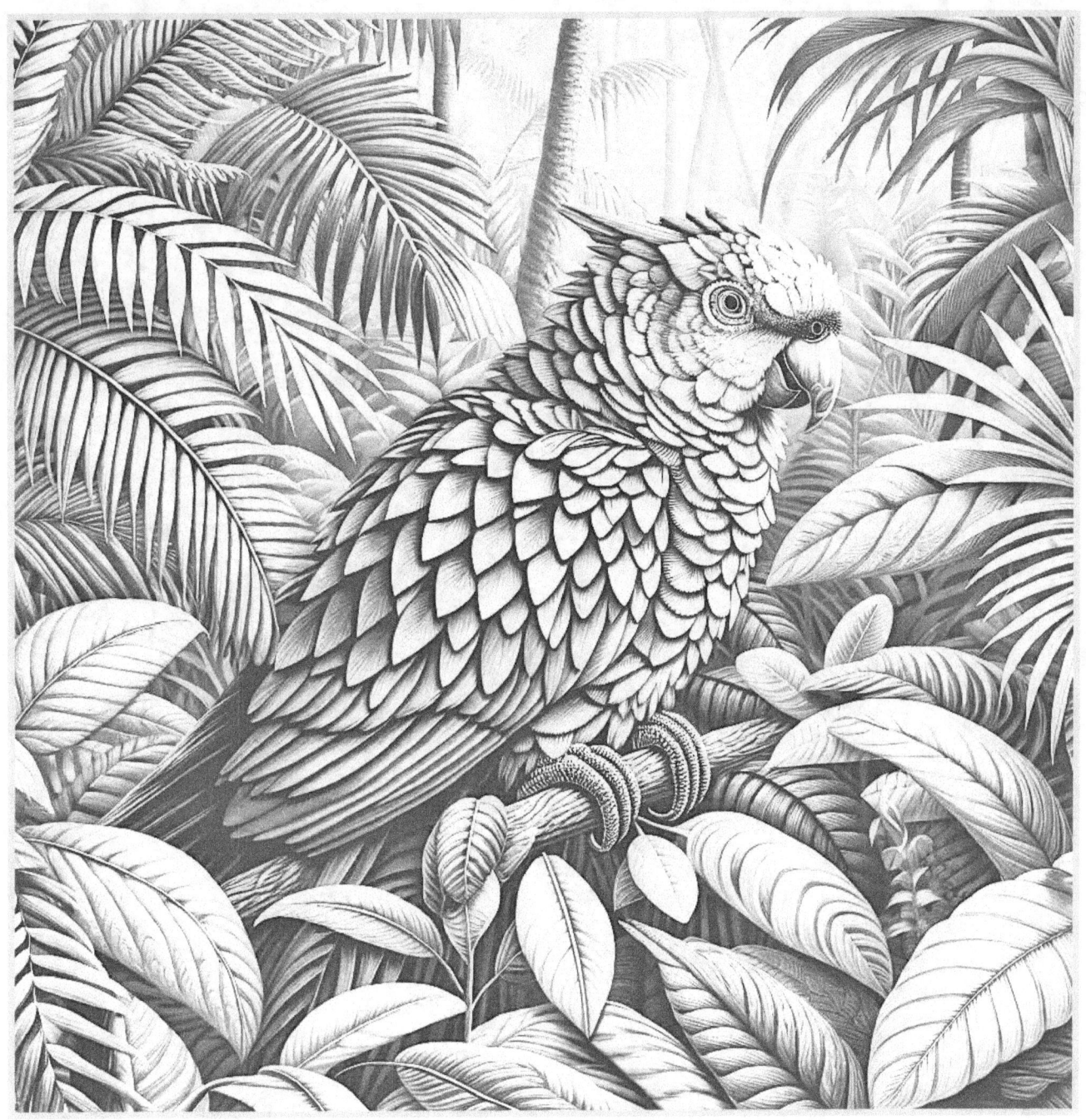

Nightjar

The Nightjar seamlessly merges with the forest floor, blending in perfectly amid the fallen leaves and twigs, showcasing its detailed plumage patterns.

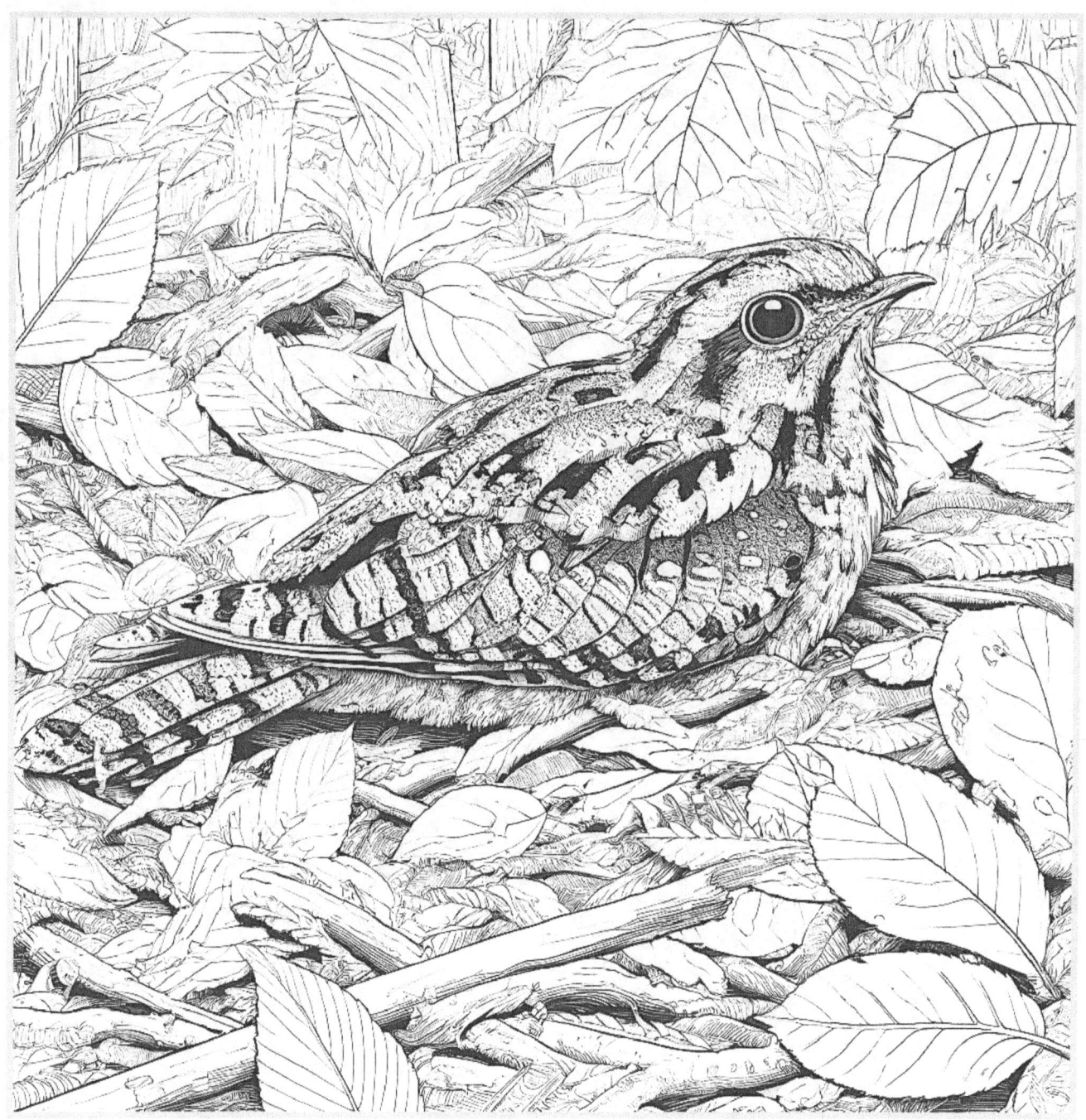

Frogmouth

Camouflaged against tree bark, the Frogmouth bird seamlessly merges with the bark, highlighting its feather patterns against the tree's texture.

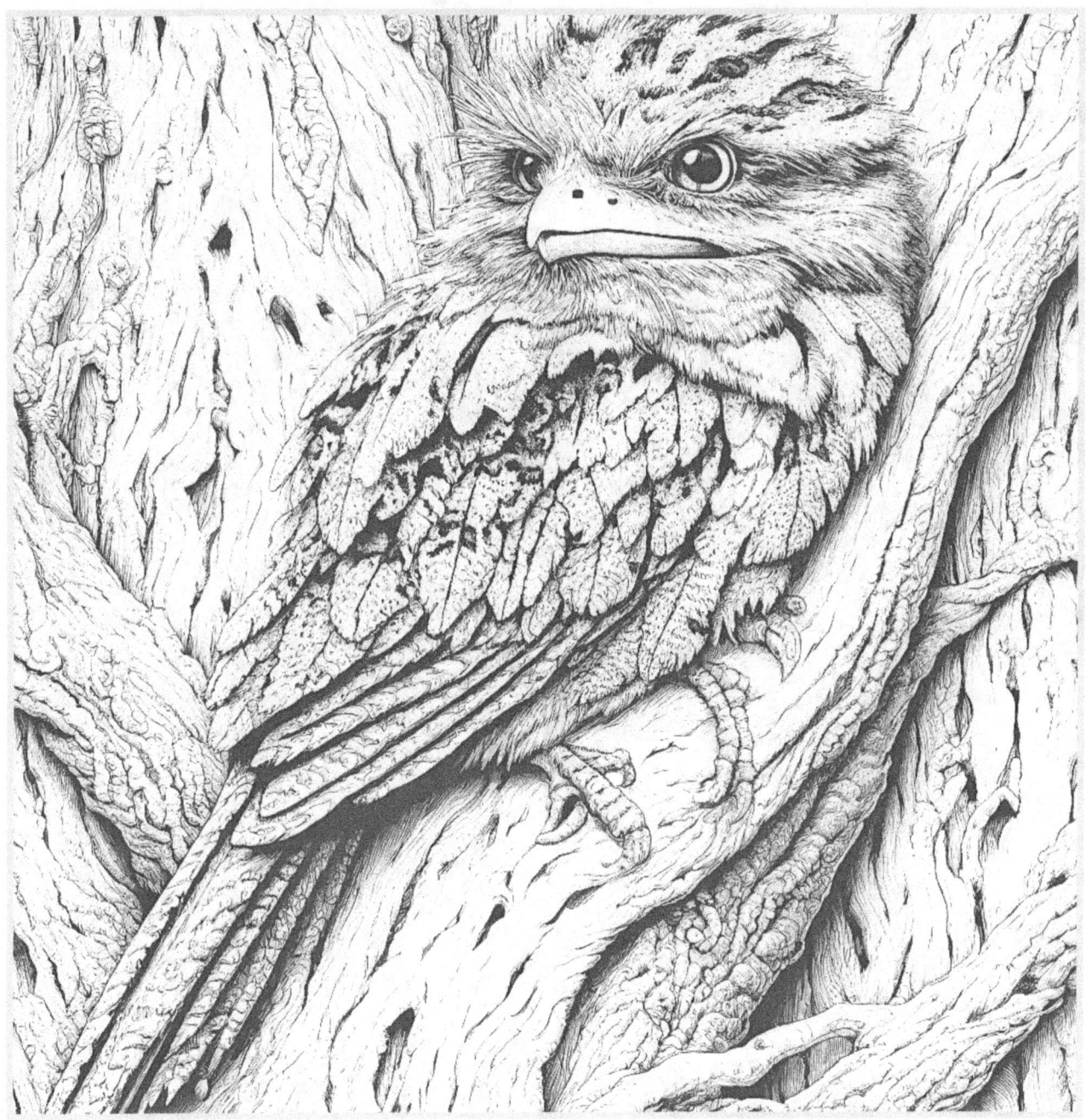

Mossy Leaf-Tailed Gecko

An example of perfect camouflage is seen in a Mossy Leaf-Tailed Gecko, which seamlessly blends into moss and foliage. This highlights its leaf-like patterns against the lush greenery of the dense moss-covered environment.

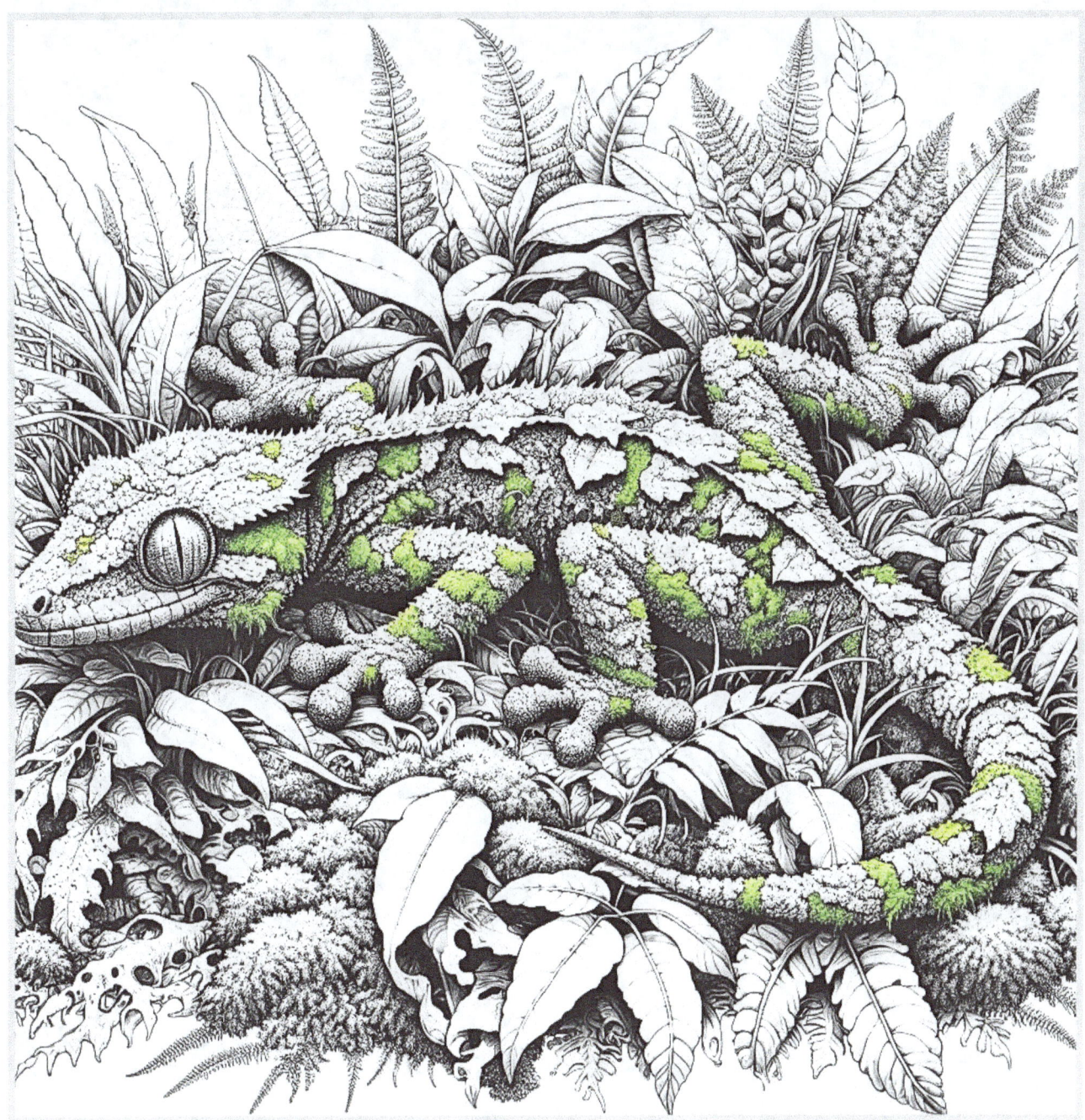

Horned Lizard

A horned lizard blends seamlessly into the sandy and rocky desert floor in this illustration, almost disappearing into its surroundings.

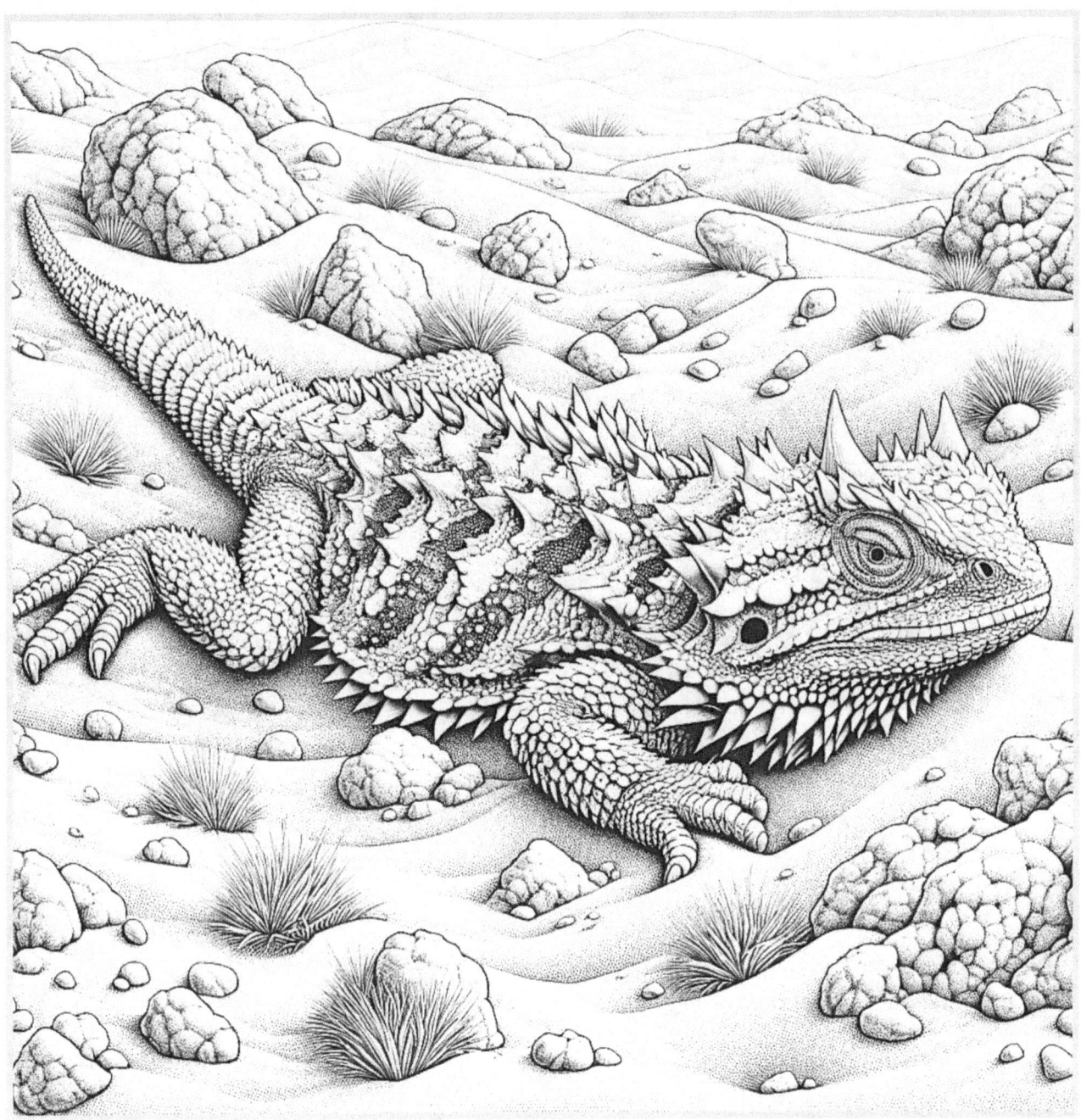

Chameleon

Among lush green leaves, a Chameleon skillfully disguises itself, demonstrating its impressive talent for blending in. This striking image not only showcases the Chameleon's color-changing abilities but also captures the vibrant foliage of its natural environment, making it a standout addition to your gallery collection.

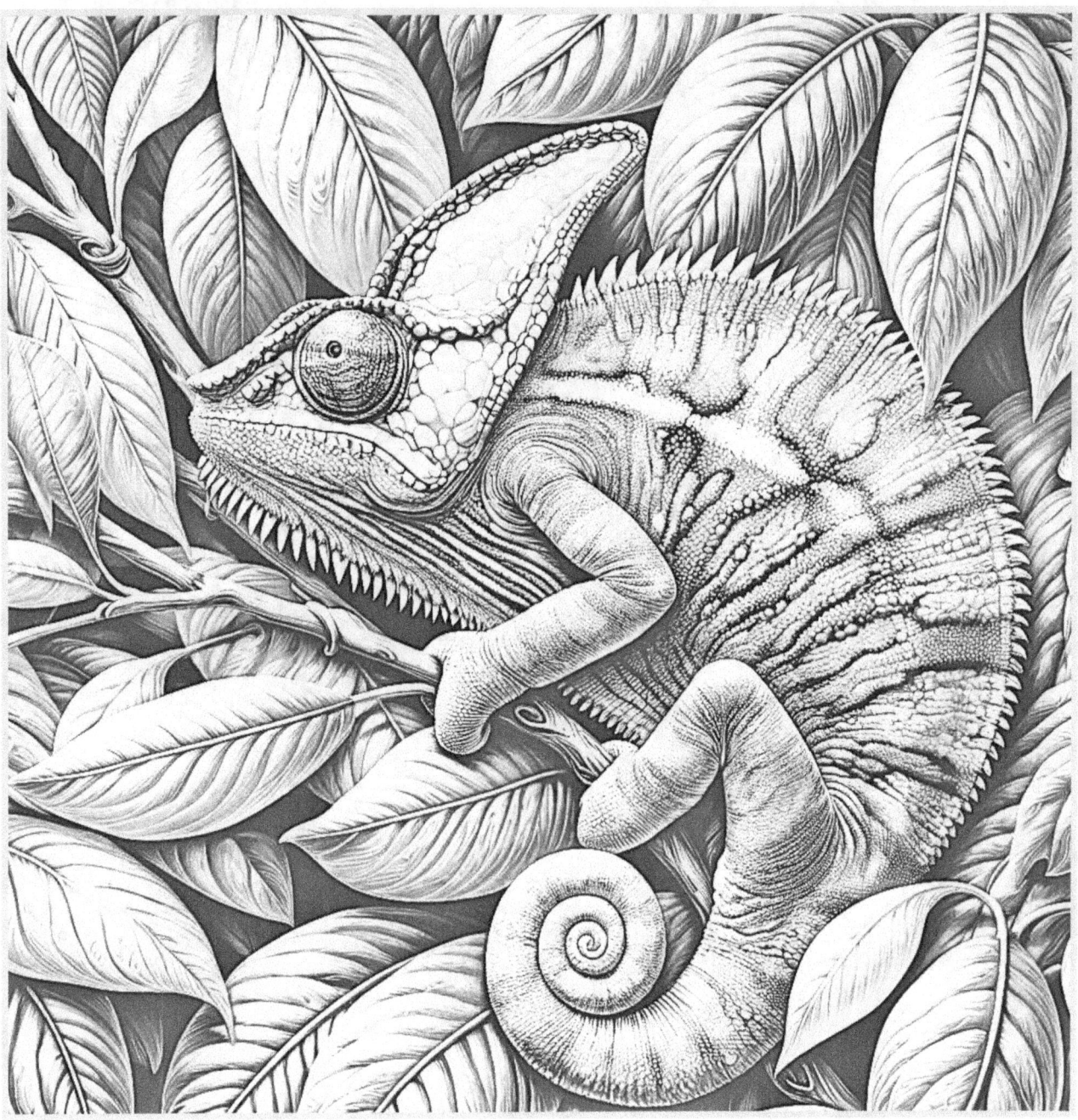

Copperhead Snake

Among the leaf litter and debris in its woodland habitat, a Copperhead Snake blends seamlessly with the forest floor, highlighting its scales against the textures of the surrounding leaves and twigs.

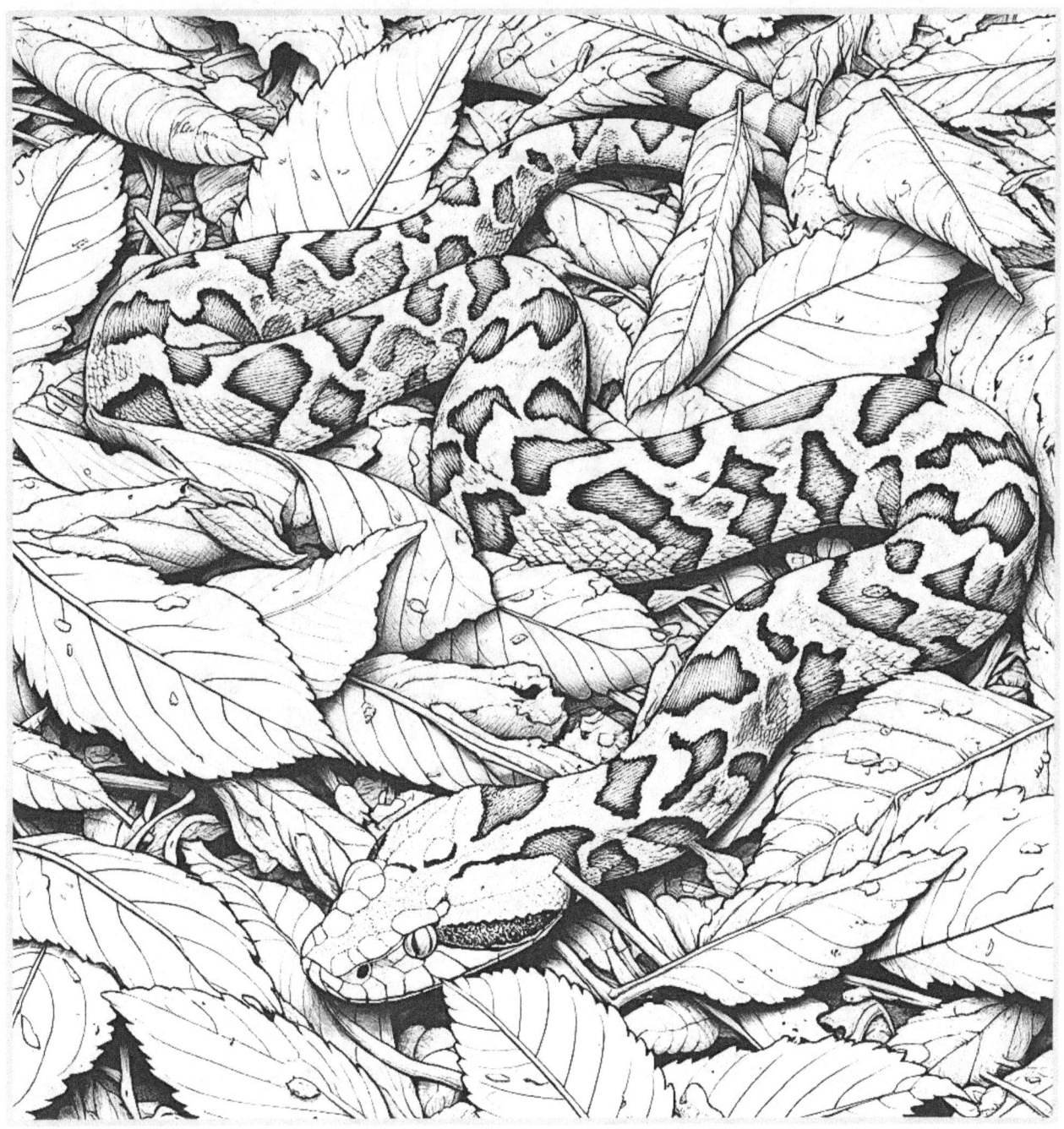

Desert Tortoise

Hidden within the dry landscape and limited plant life of the desert, the tortoise seamlessly merges with its surroundings, showcasing its speckled, earth-colored shell against the rocky desert ground.

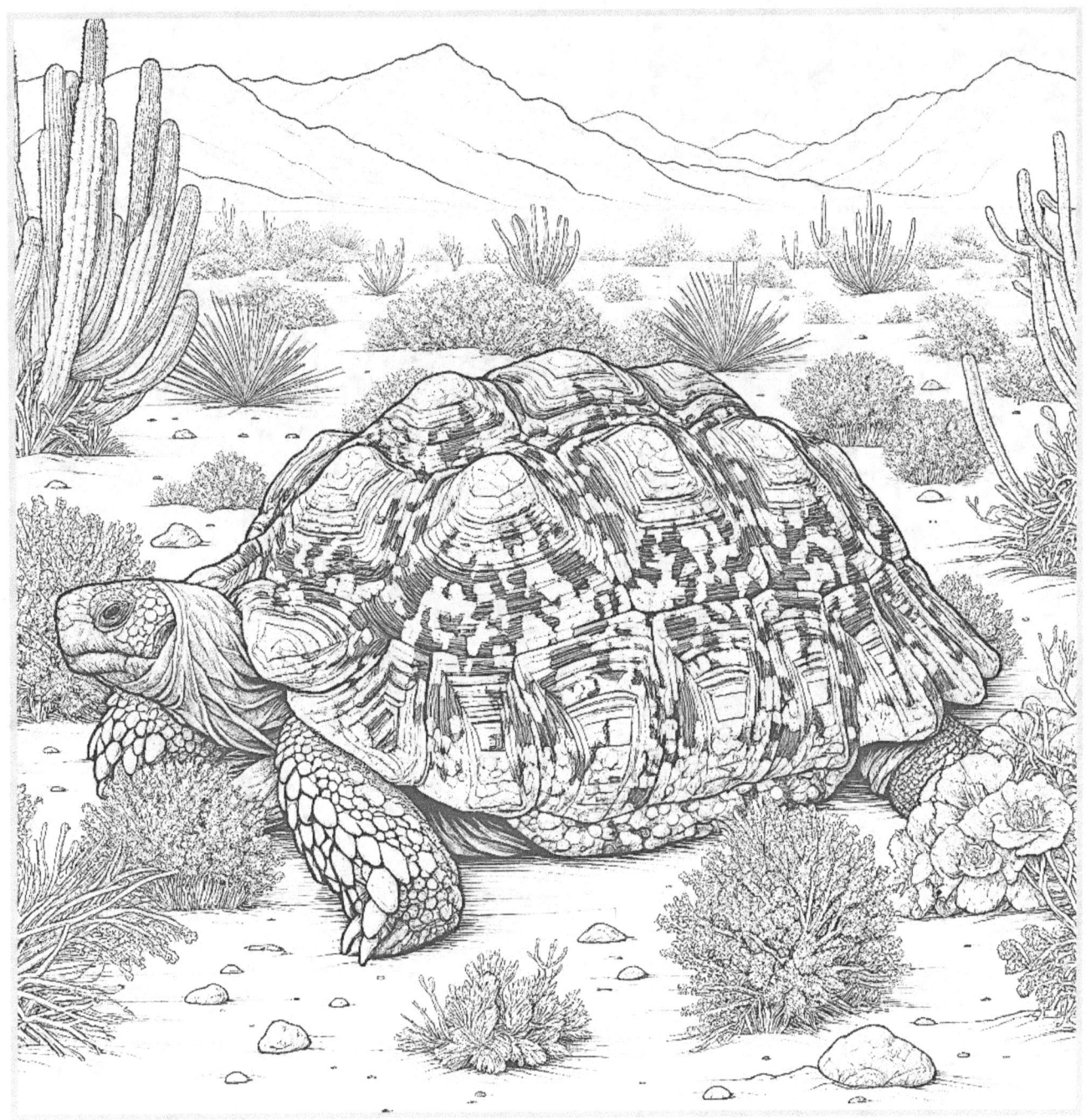

Green Sea Turtle

In a vibrant underwater realm filled with seaweed and coral, the Green Sea Turtle blends in effortlessly. This mesmerizing sight demonstrates how the turtle skillfully hides among its surroundings, revealing its shell patterns amidst the colorful underwater flora.

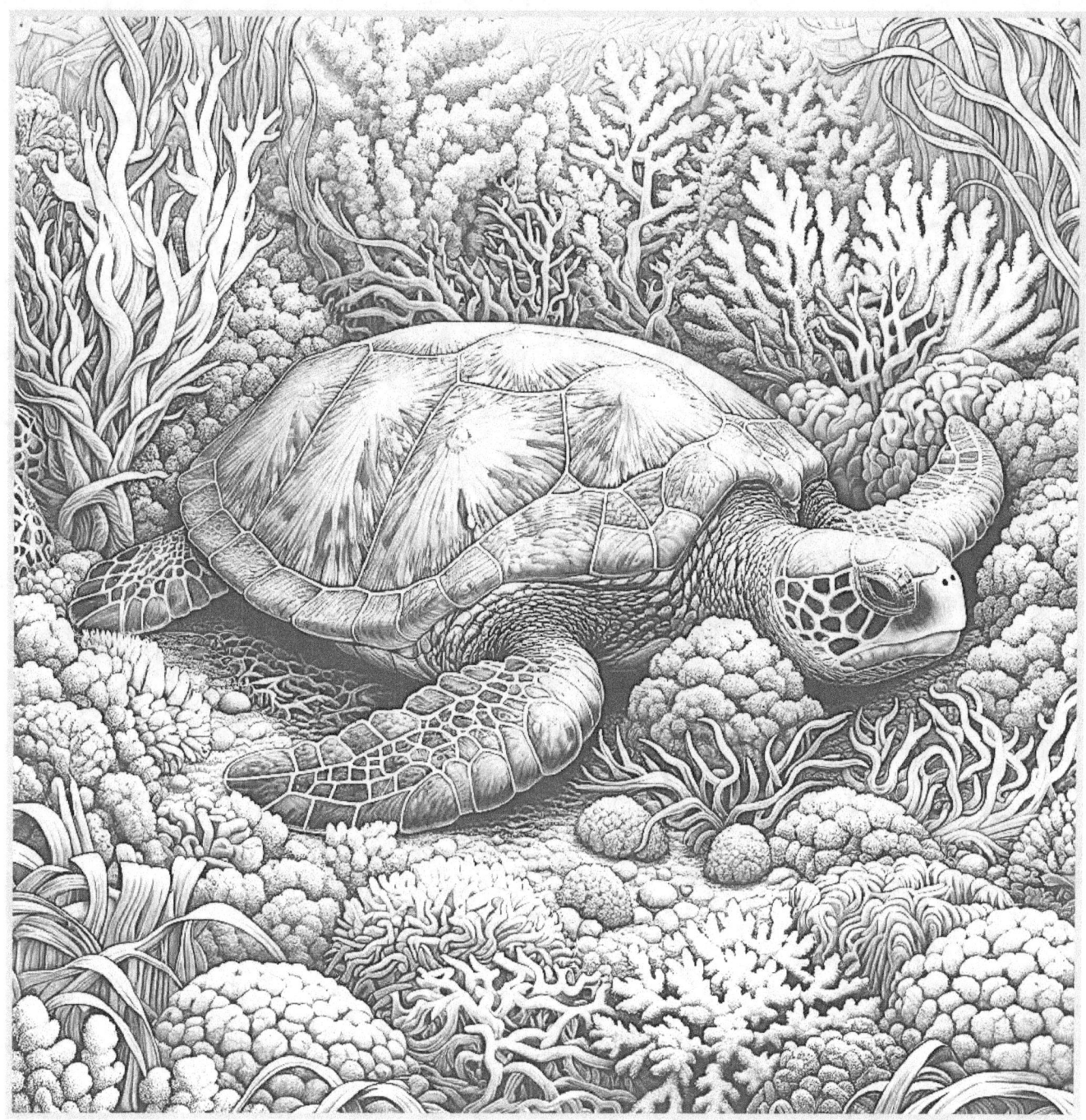

Ghost Pipefish

In the underwater realm of seagrass, the Ghost Pipefish stands out for its adept camouflage skills, effortlessly merging with its surroundings to unveil its delicate shape amidst the lively seagrass ecosystem.

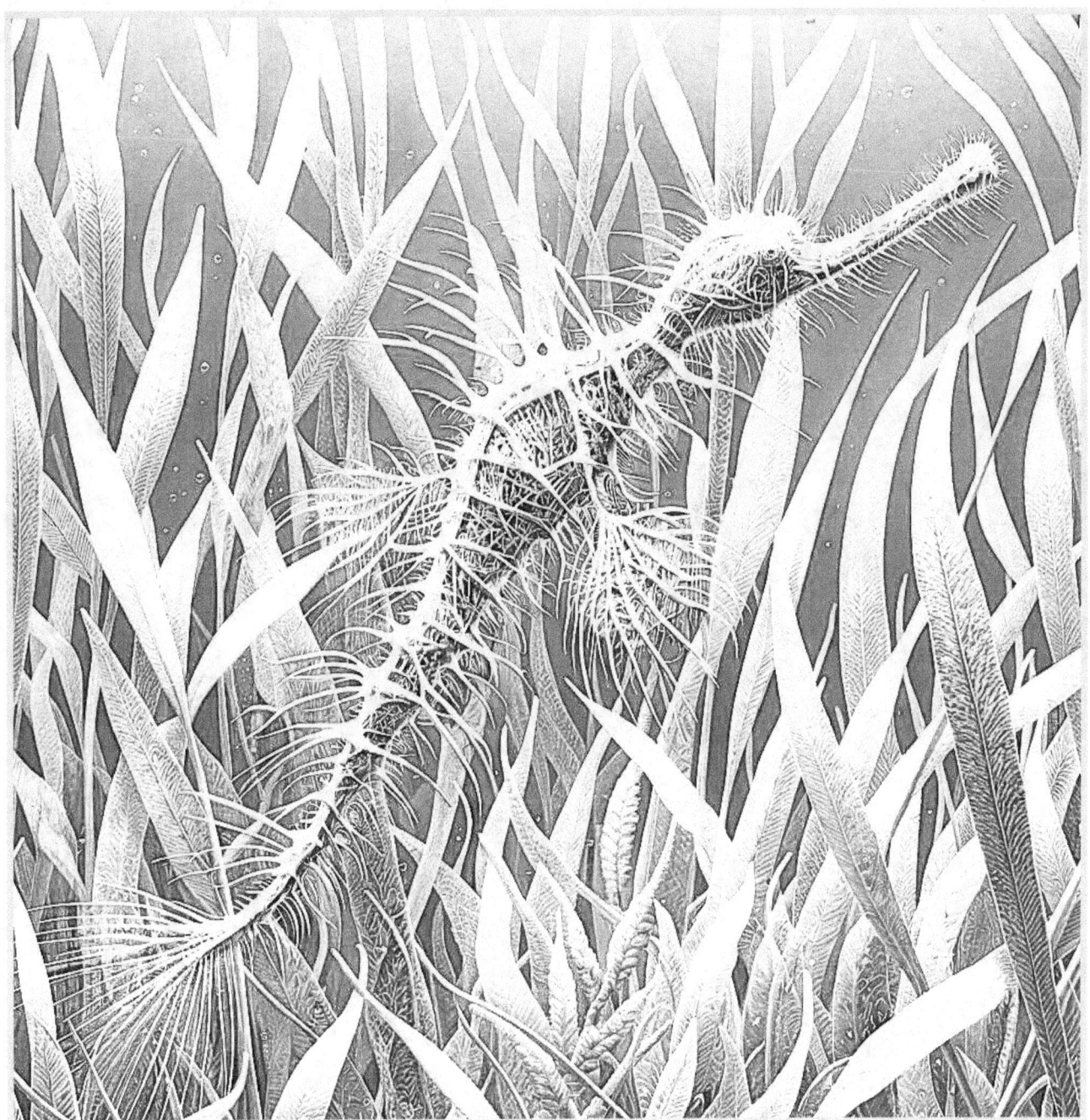

Octopus

The octopus excels at mimicking the textures of coral and seaweed, creating a mesmerizing and complex image for coloring.

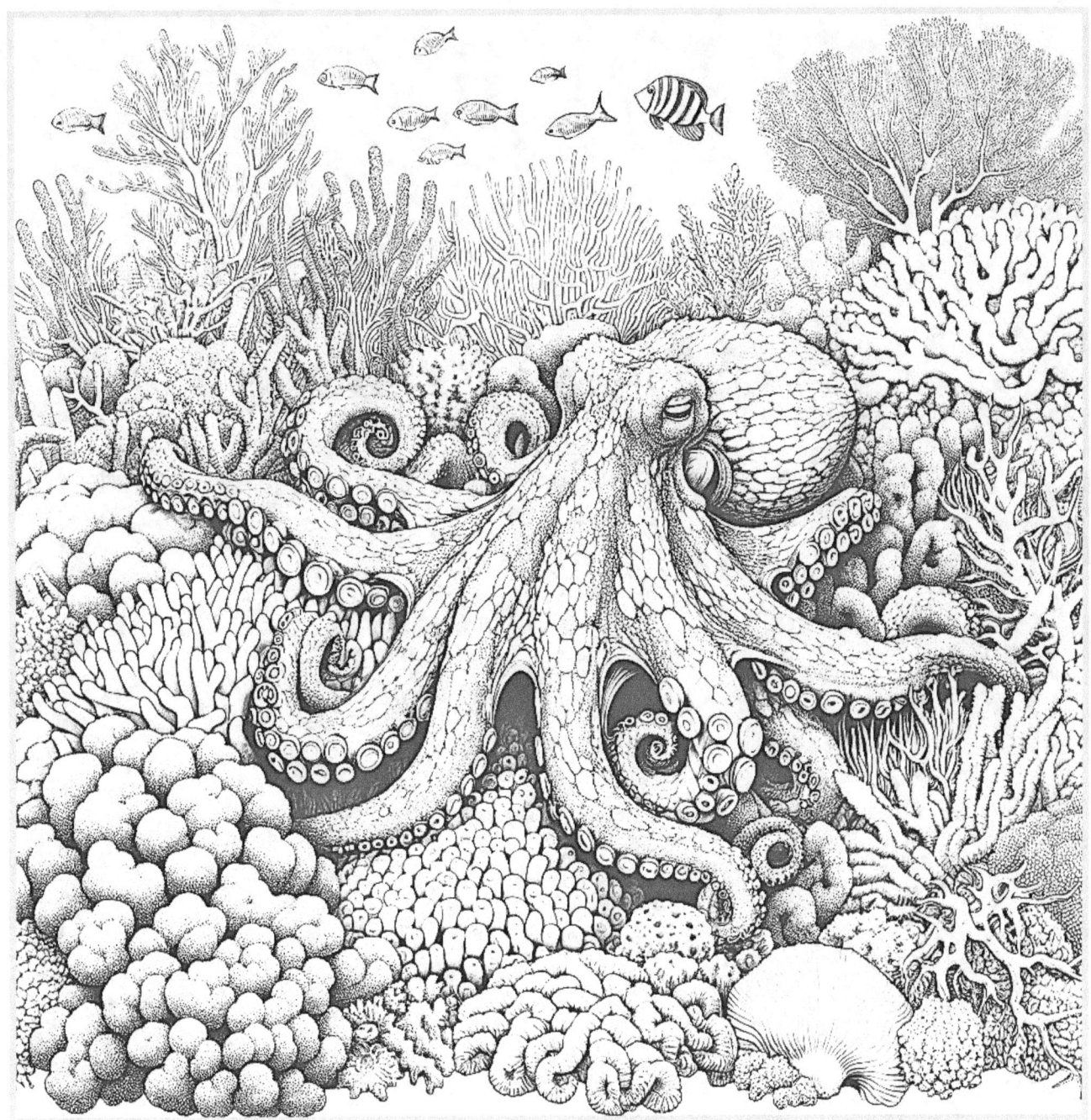

Wobbegong Shark

The Wobbegong Shark expertly camouflages itself within the rocky and sandy seabed, displaying its intricate patterns and blending with the diverse textures of the underwater surroundings.

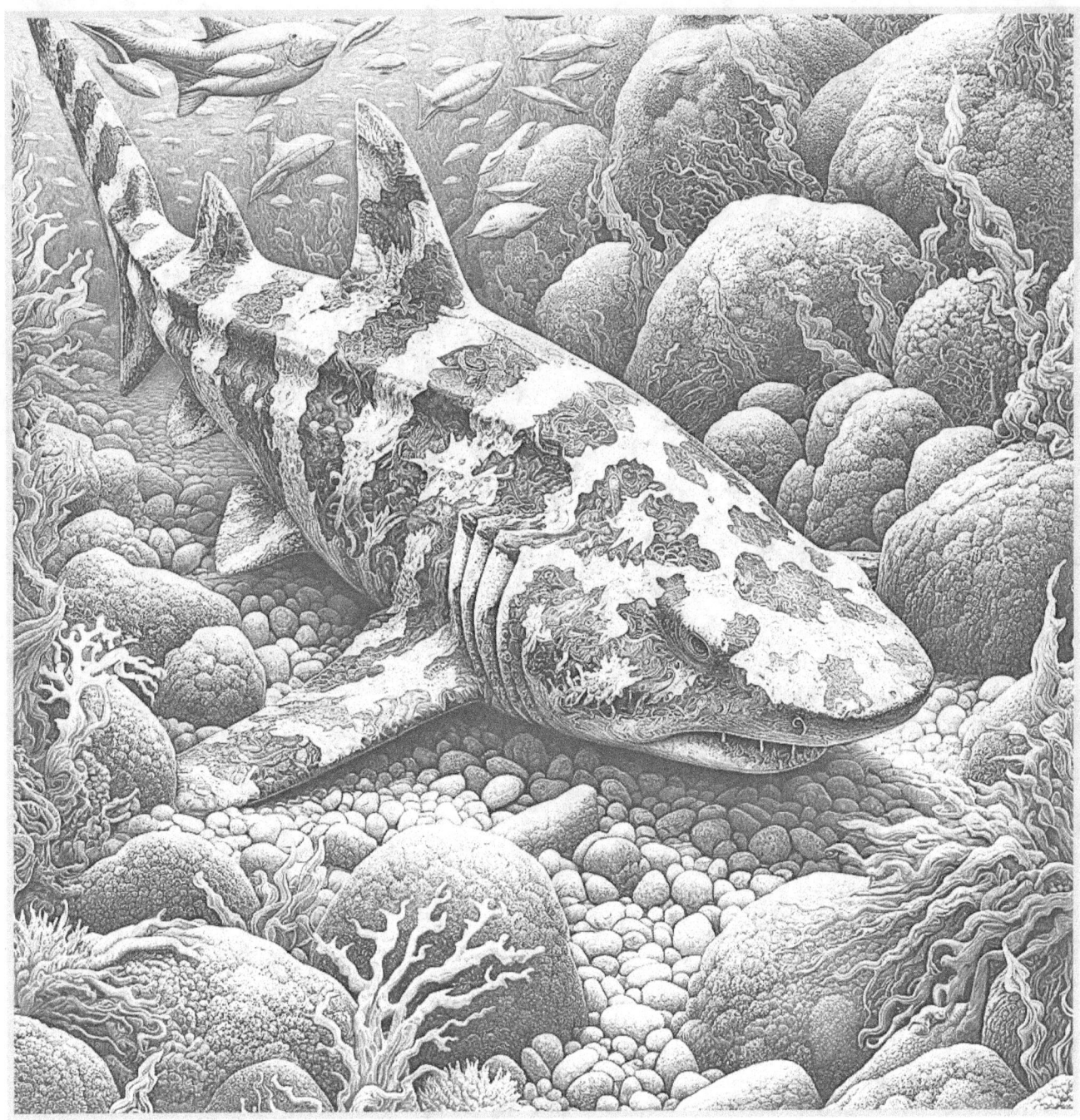

Stone Flounder

The Stone Flounder, hidden on the rocky ocean floor, seamlessly merges with the stones and pebbles, utilizing intricate features such as algae and small sea creatures to amplify its camouflage.

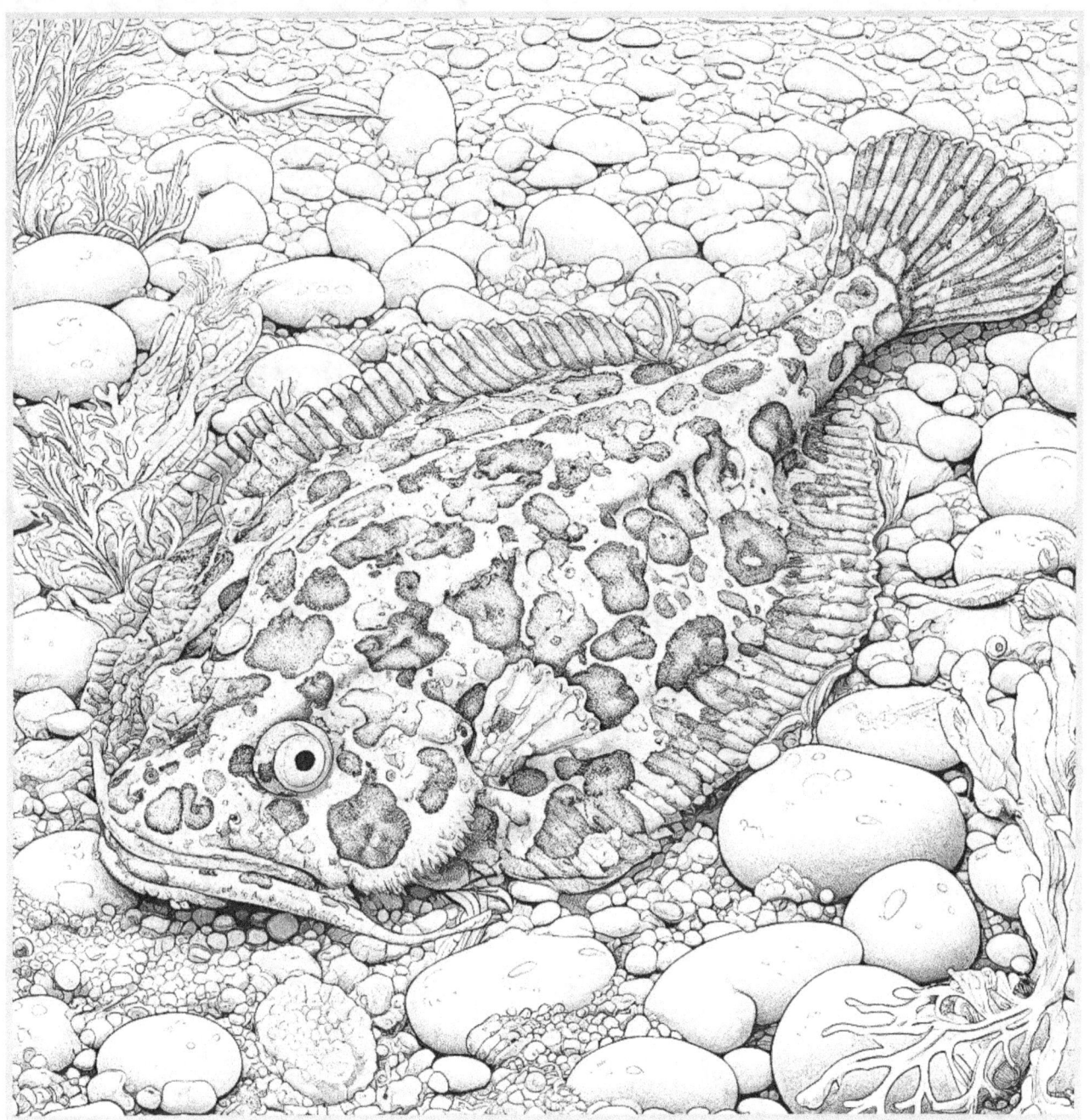

Leafy Sea Dragon

Among the seaweed and kelp, the Leafy Sea Dragon expertly camouflages itself within its underwater environment. Its leaf-like appearance harmonizes with the textured aquatic flora, creating a stunning blend with its surroundings.

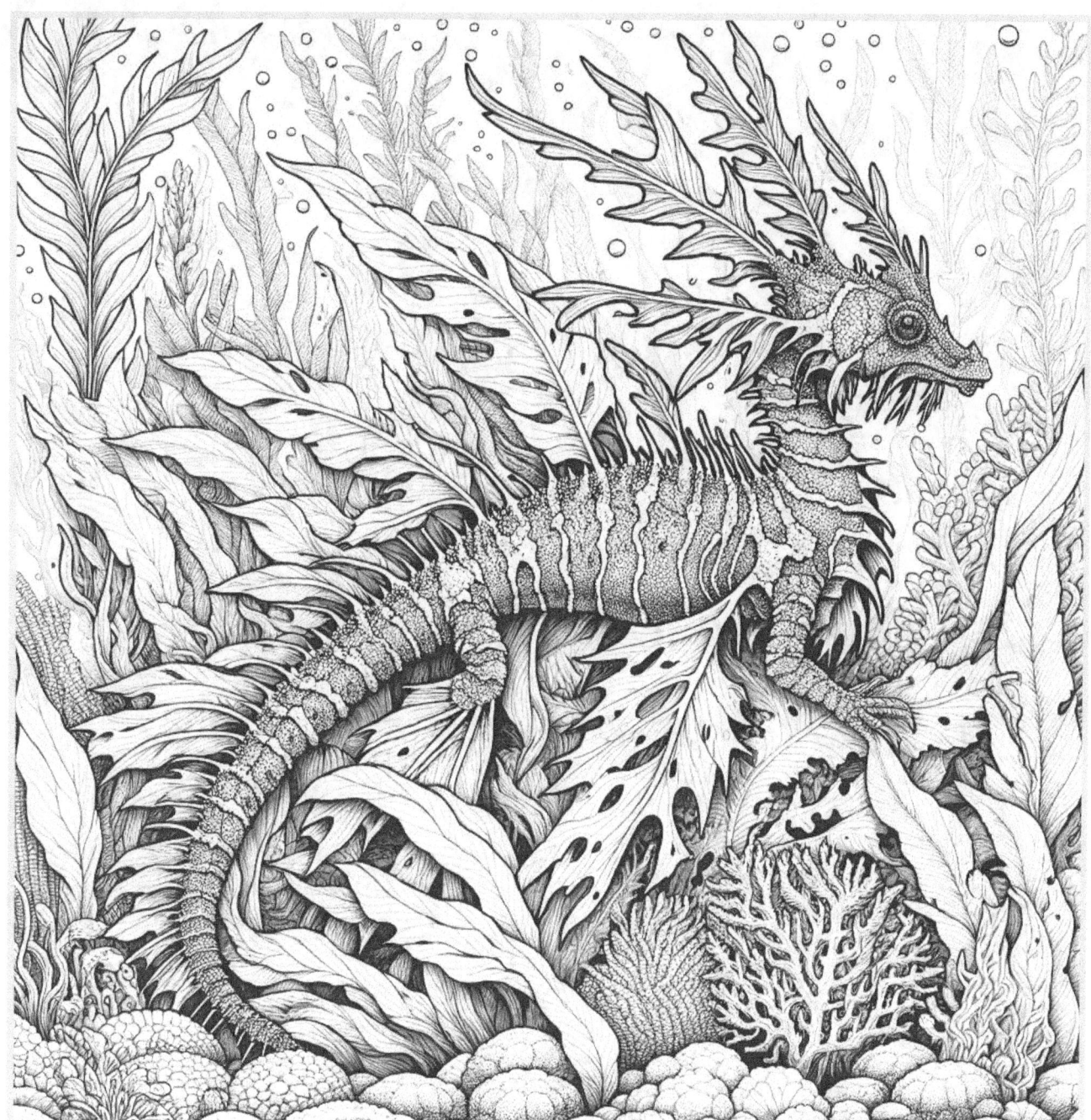

Arctic Hare

The Arctic Hare seamlessly blends into the snowy landscape, highlighting its fur texture against the icy terrain.

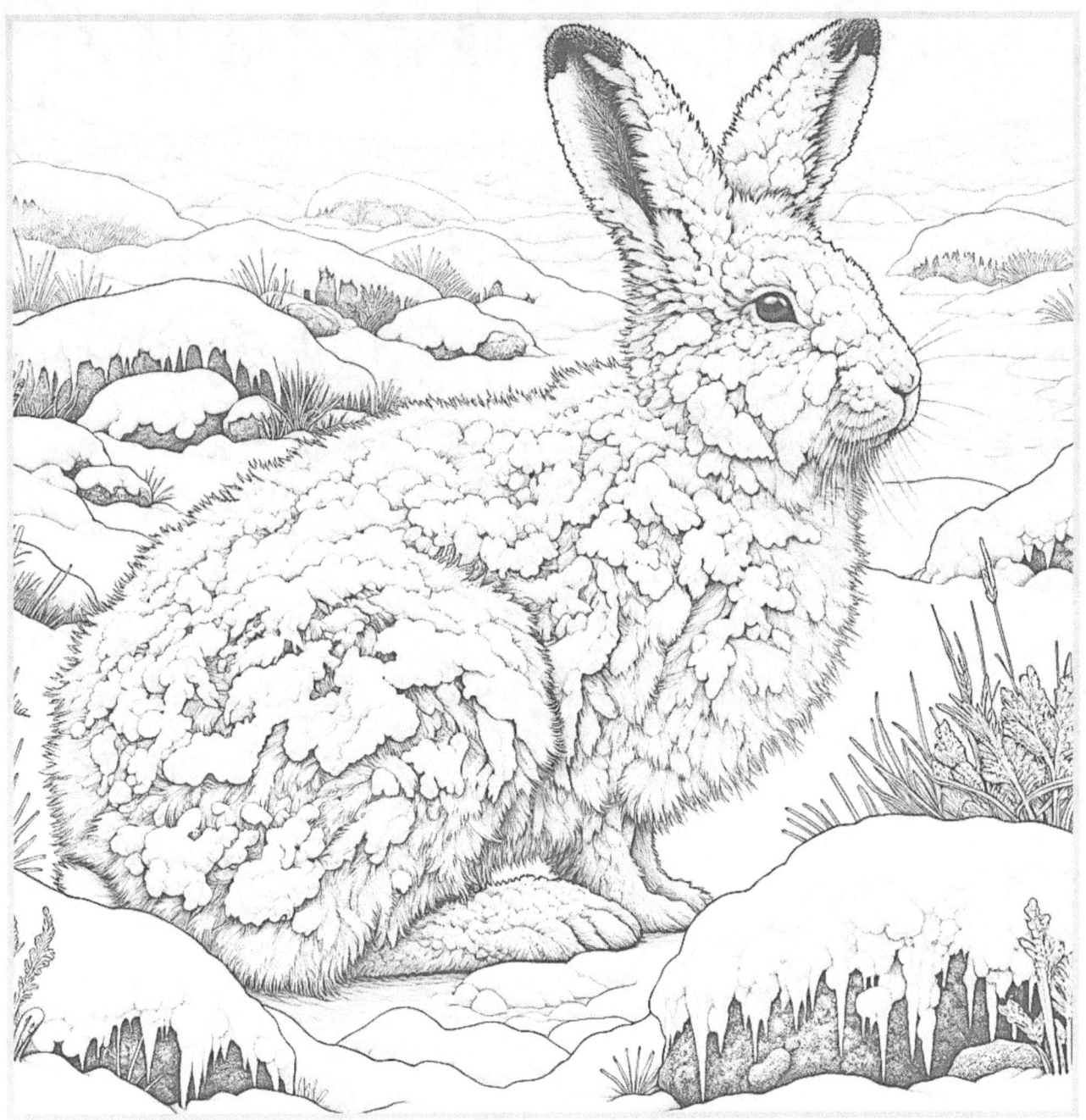

Snow Leopard

The snow leopard is highly skilled at blending into its snowy mountain habitat. Its fur pattern seamlessly merges with the rocky and snowy landscape, presenting a fascinating and complex coloring illusion.

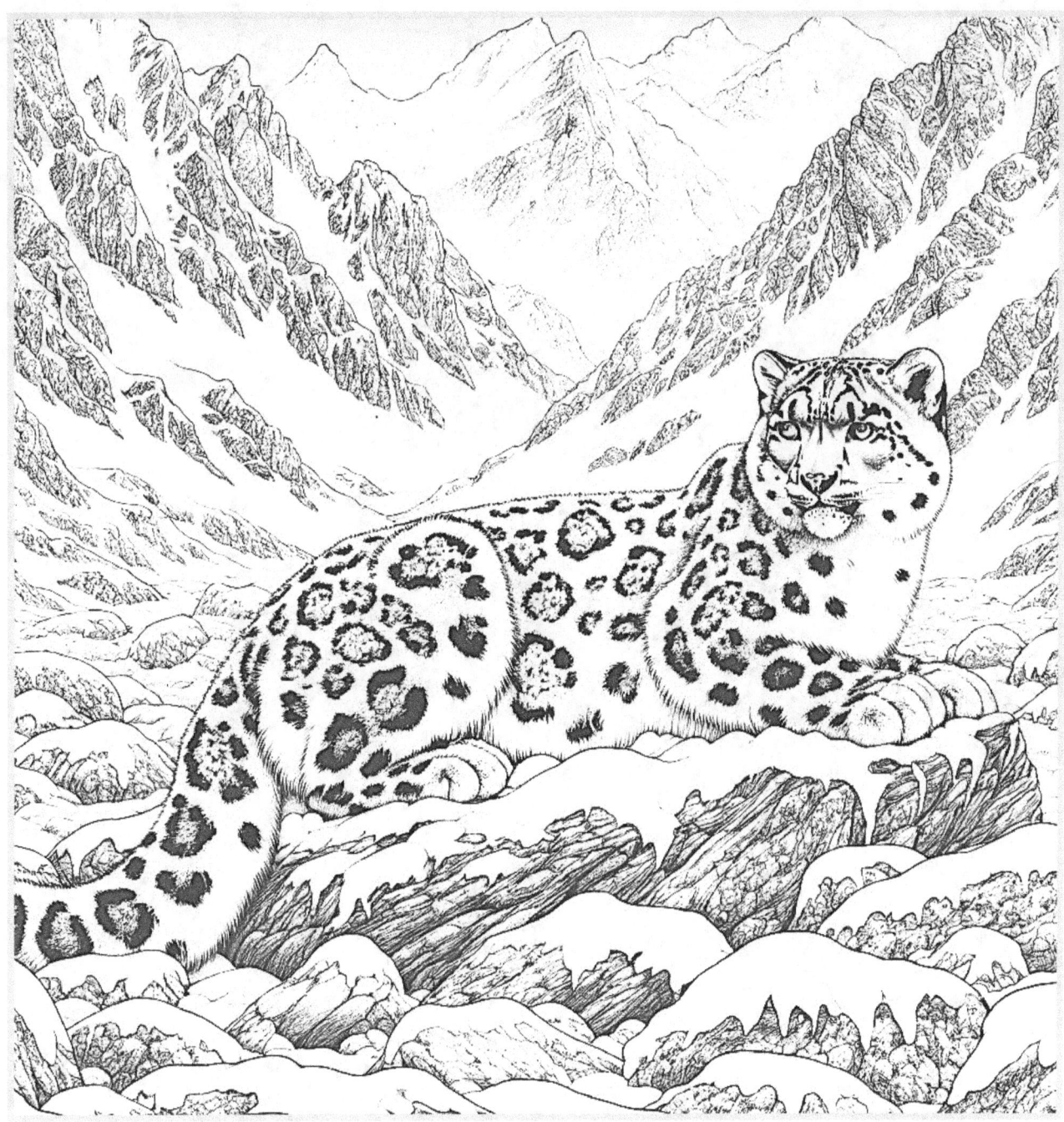

Ocelot

An ocelot effortlessly merges into the undergrowth of the rainforest, displaying its effective camouflage within the surroundings.

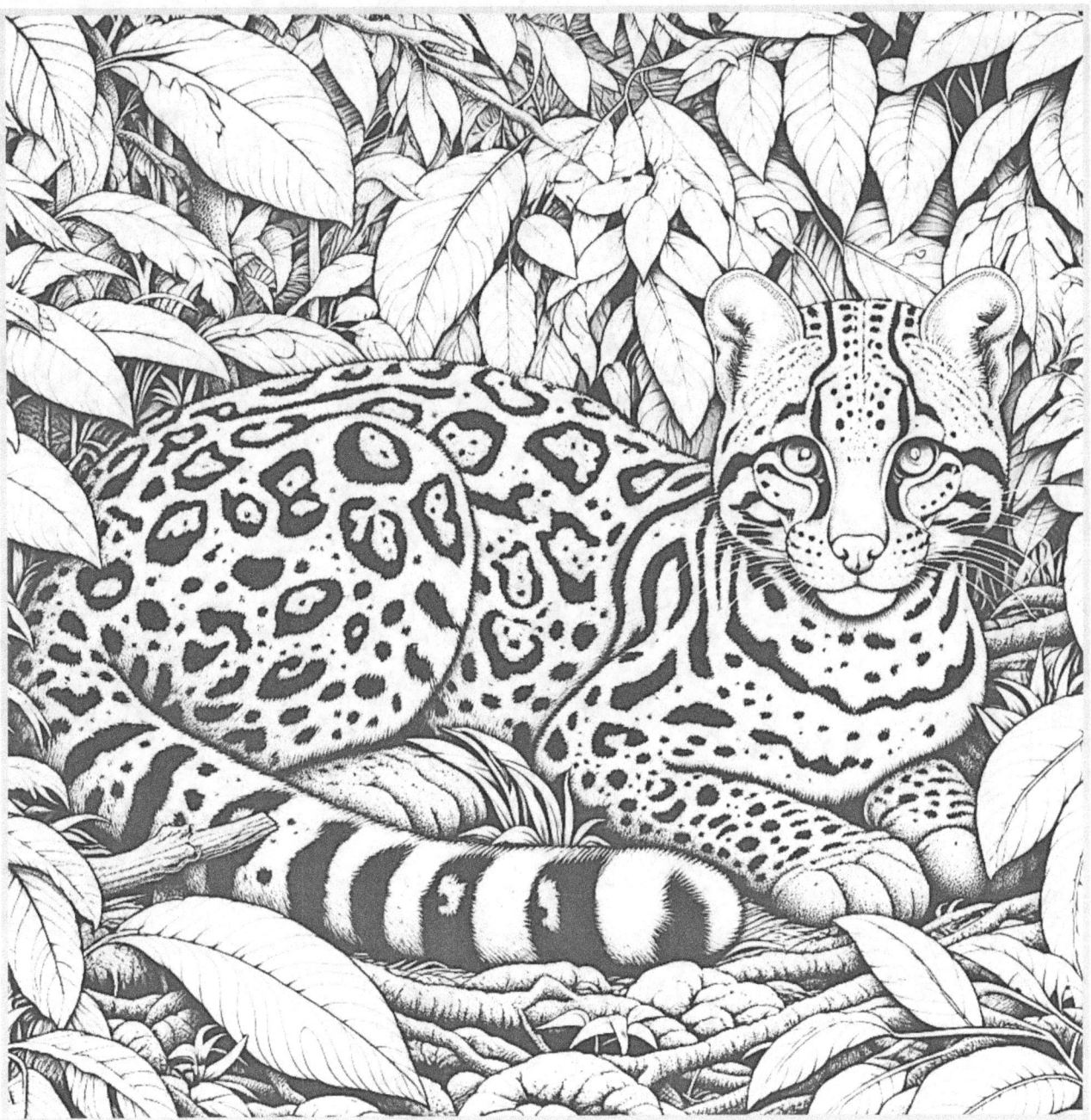

Sand Cat

The Sand Cat effortlessly merges with the sandy desert dunes, almost vanishing amid its surroundings, showcasing its light coat and sandy textures.

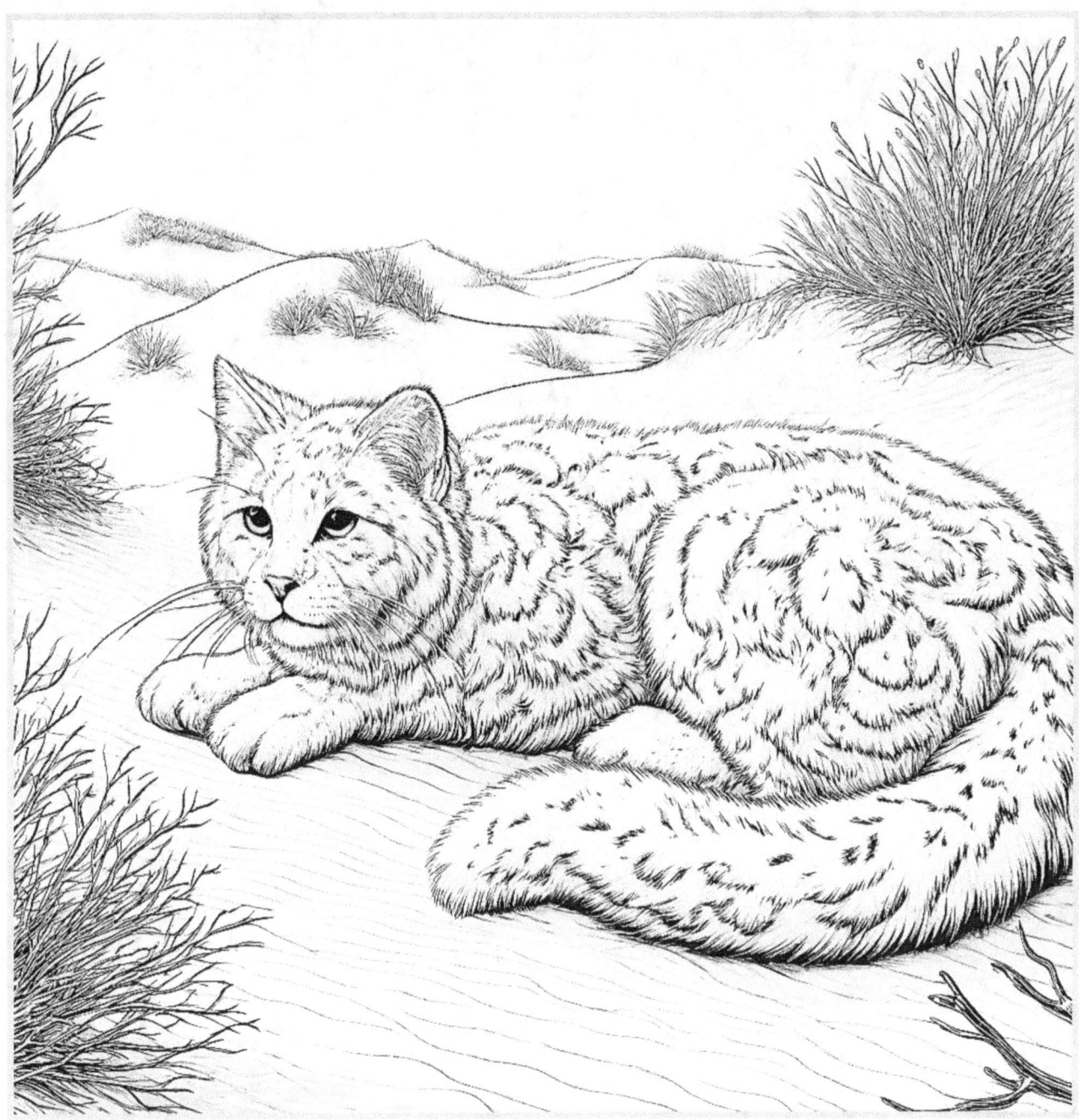

Tiger

A tiger seamlessly blends into the dense jungle undergrowth, as its distinctive striped fur merges with the varying shadows and light patterns of the forest.

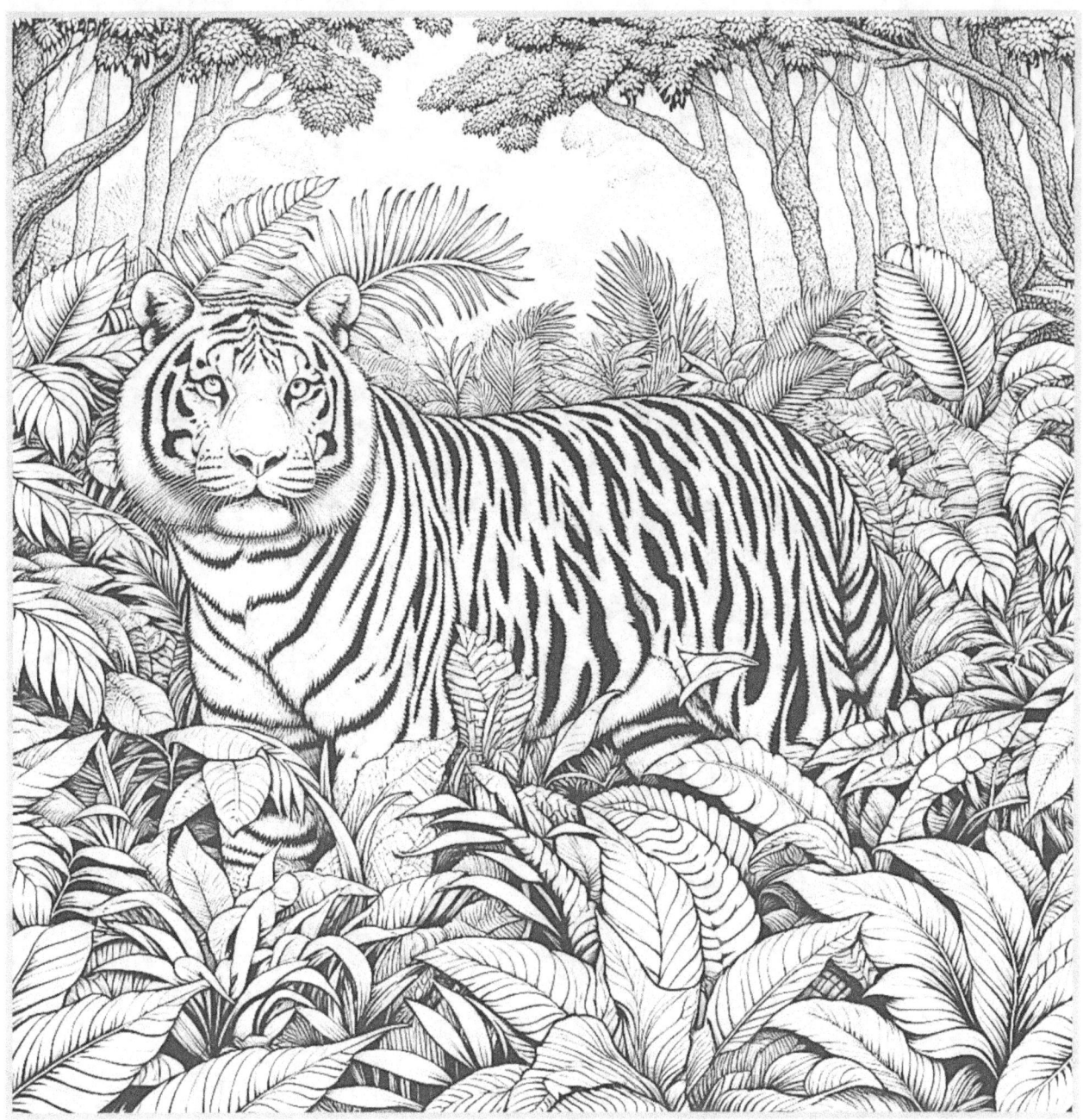

Cheetah

The cheetah hides within the savannah grassland, effortlessly blending into the tall, dry grass. Its distinct spotted coat easily merges with the surrounding vegetation, offering efficient camouflage.

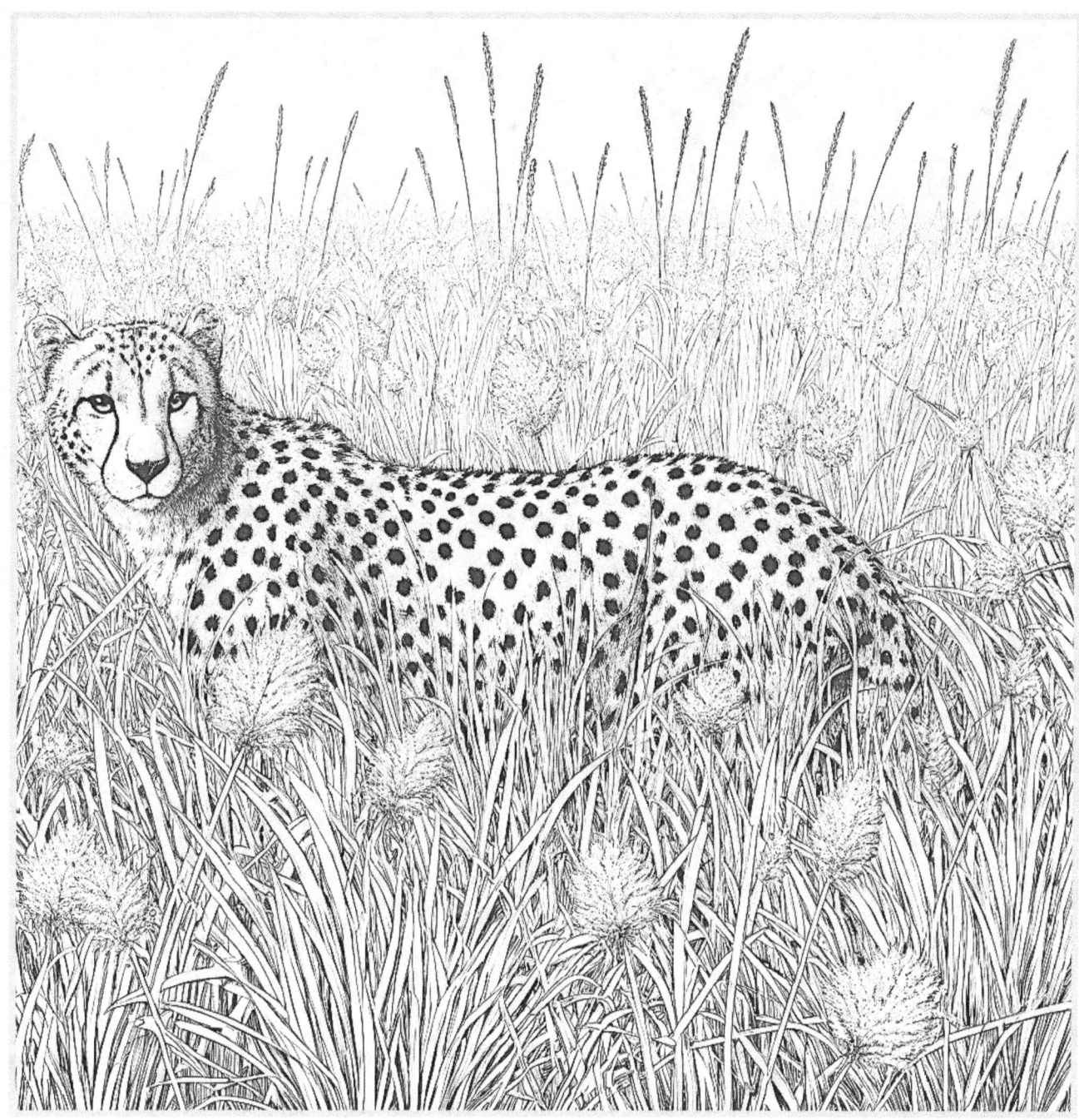

Jaguar

A Jaguar, hidden in a lush rainforest, effortlessly blends into the vibrant undergrowth. Its coat, decorated with rosette patterns, reflects the dance of sunlight and shadows within the forest.

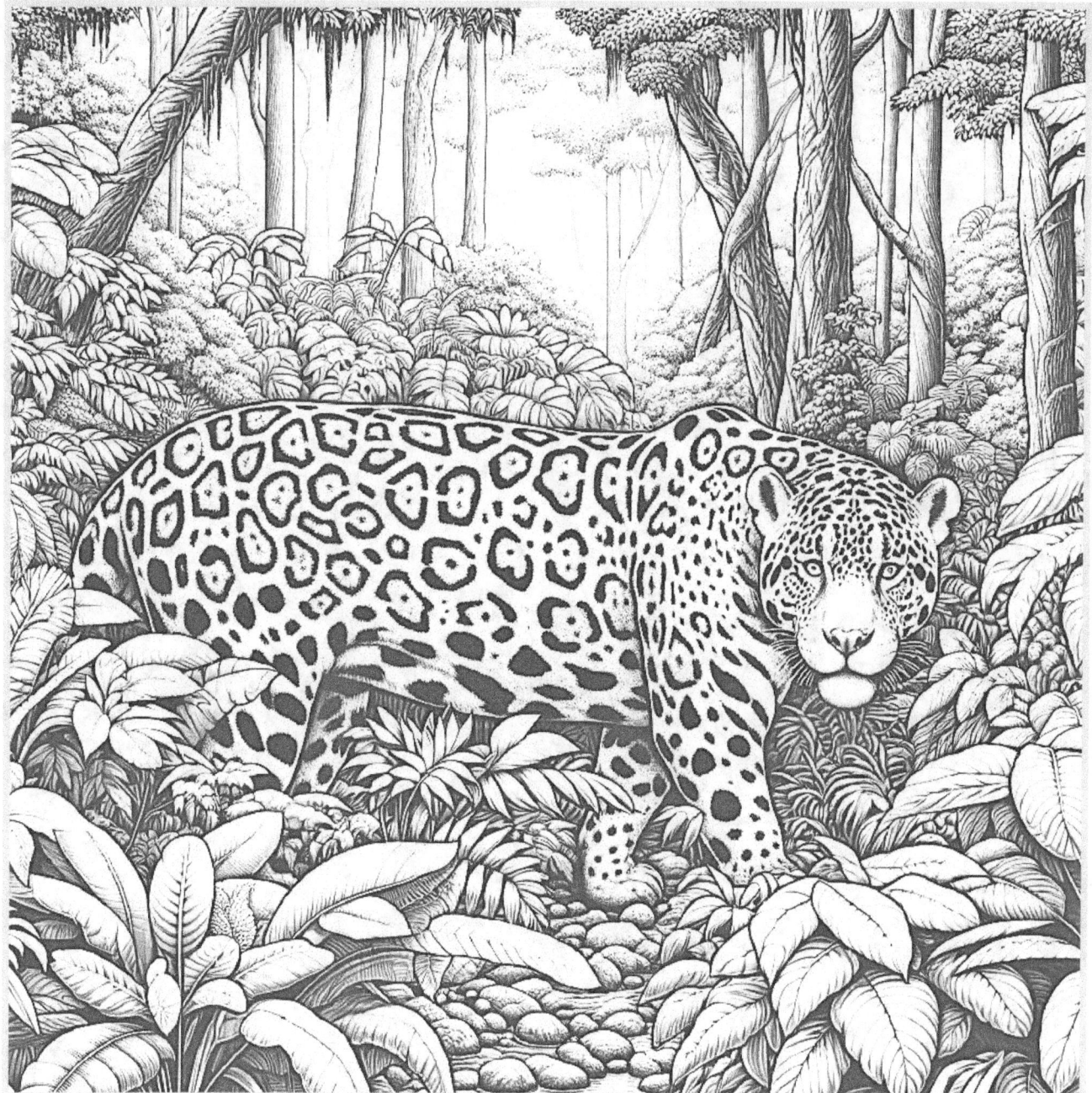

Fennec Fox

In the desert, the Fennec Fox blends in perfectly with its unique large ears and sandy-colored fur.

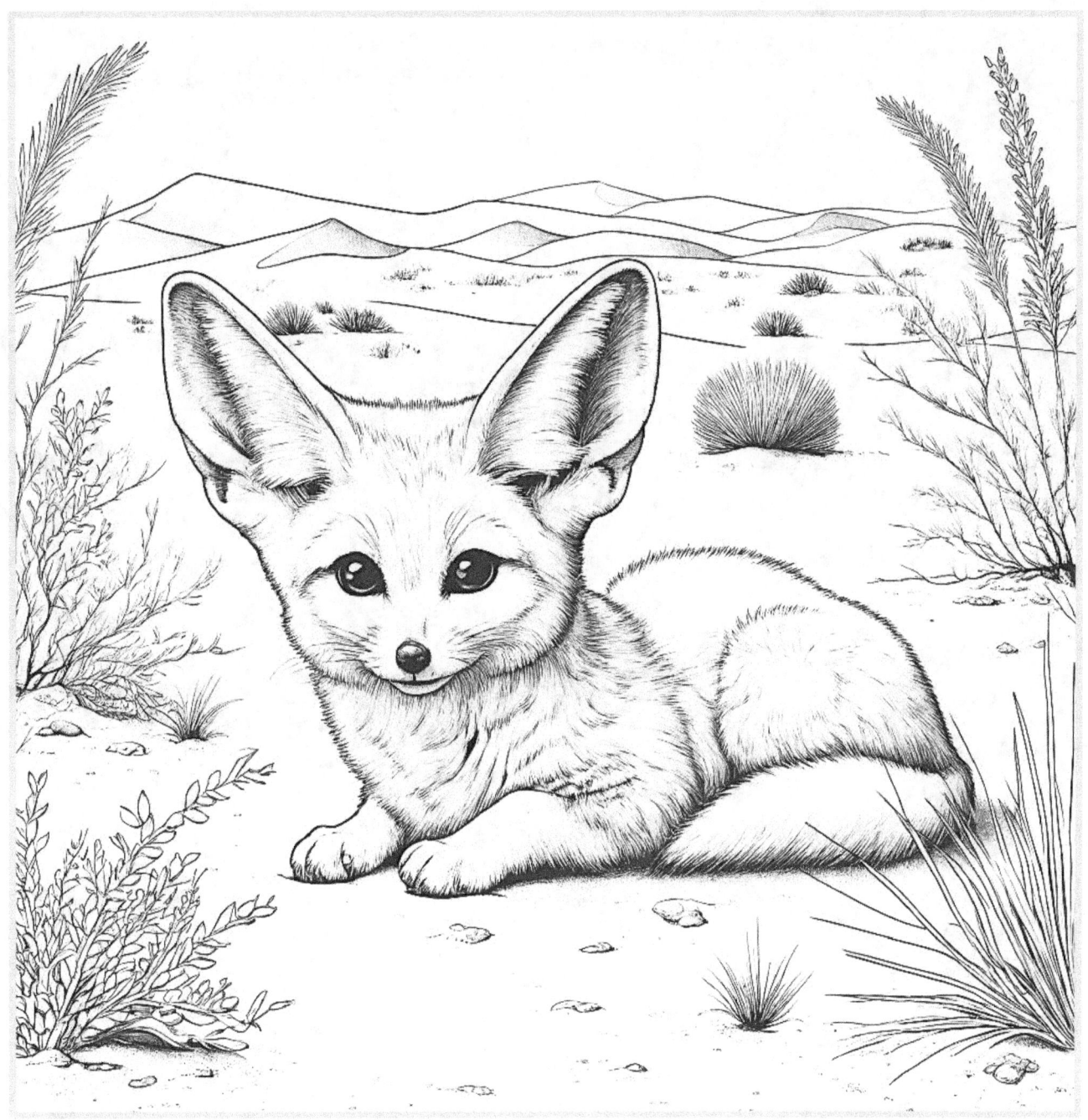

Desert Fox

The Desert Fox effortlessly merges into the sandy terrain, blending its light fur with the desert's hues.

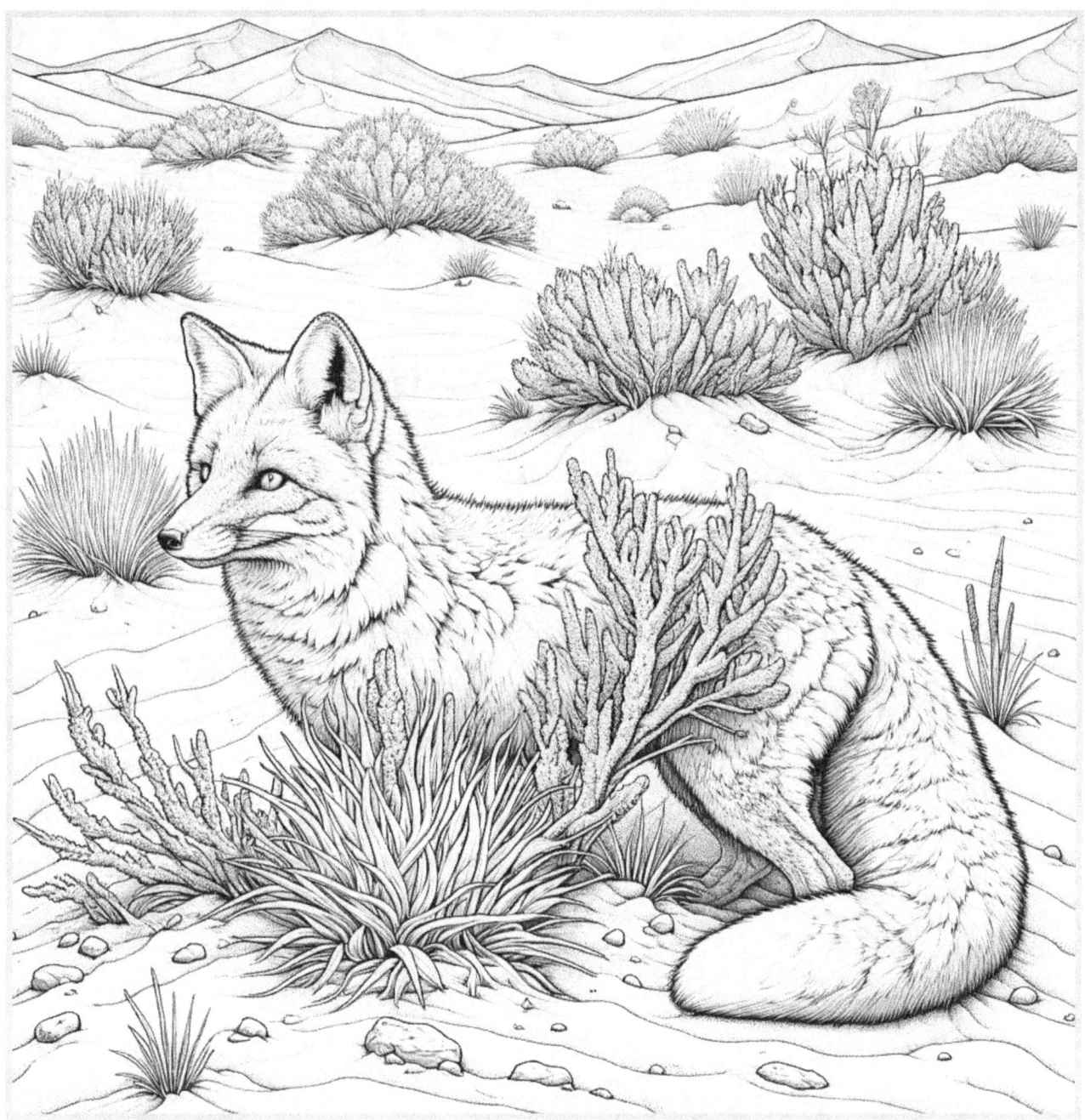

Nubian Ibex

The Nubian Ibex harmoniously blends into the rocky desert cliffs, perfectly camouflaged. The artwork illustrates the Ibex's seamless integration with its environment, emphasizing its robust physique amidst the rough terrain.

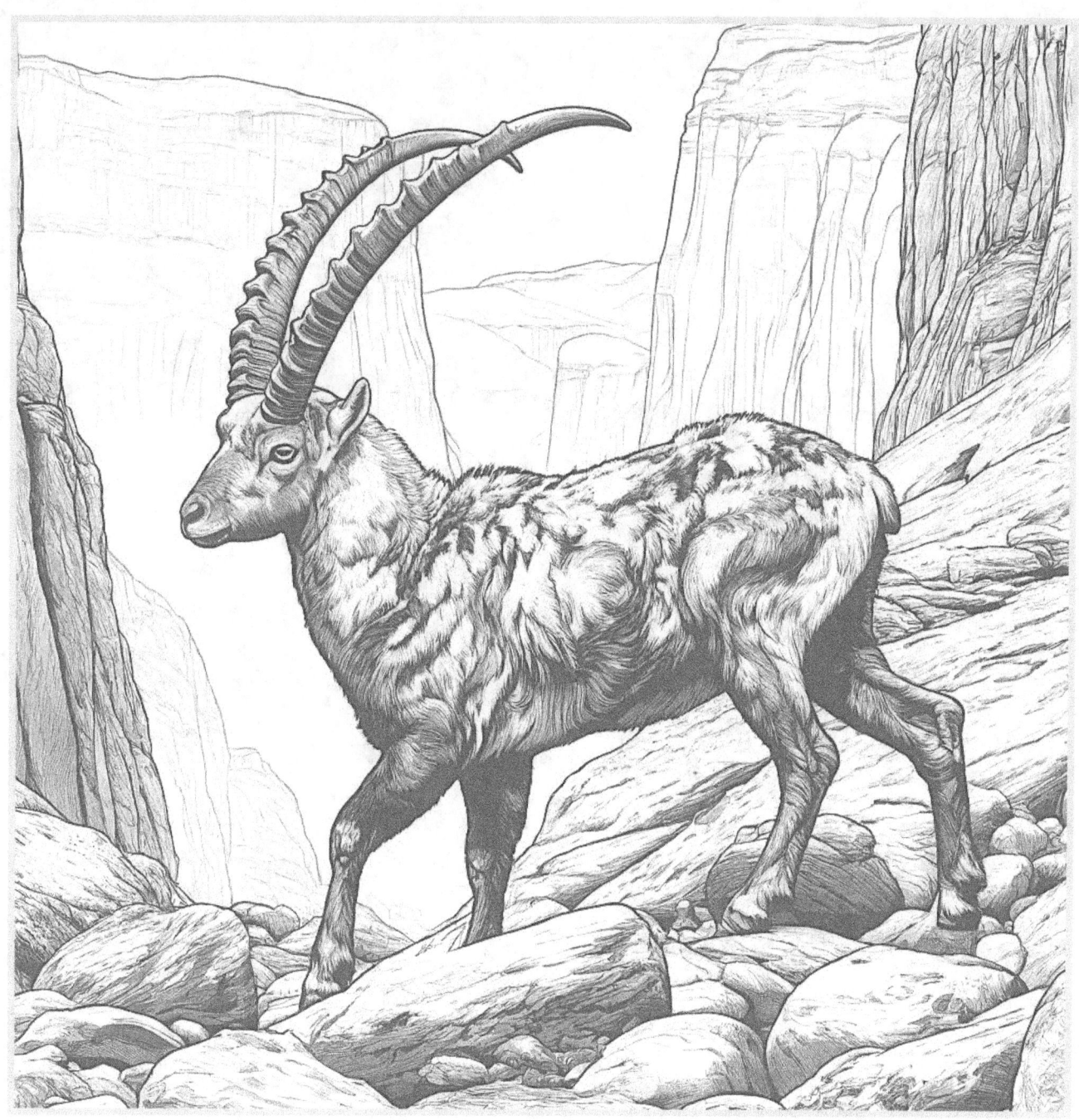

Impala

In the African savannah grasslands, an Impala expertly camouflages itself within the tall, dry grass, harmonizing with the golden hues of its environment.

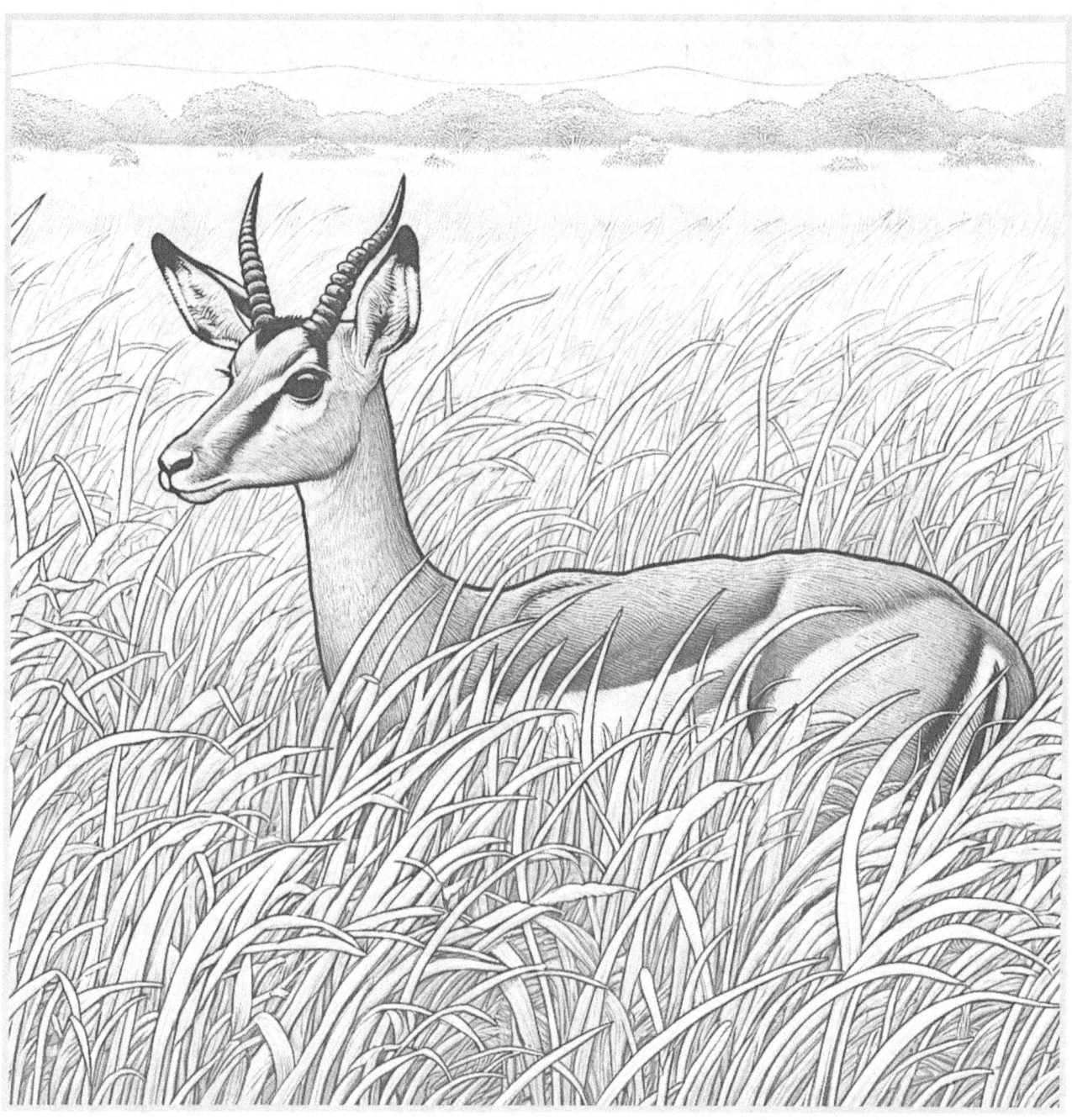

Sloth

Within the rainforest canopy, a sloth expertly conceals itself, effortlessly merging with the vibrant green vegetation. Its fur, adorned with algae, harmonizes flawlessly with the adjacent leaves and branches.

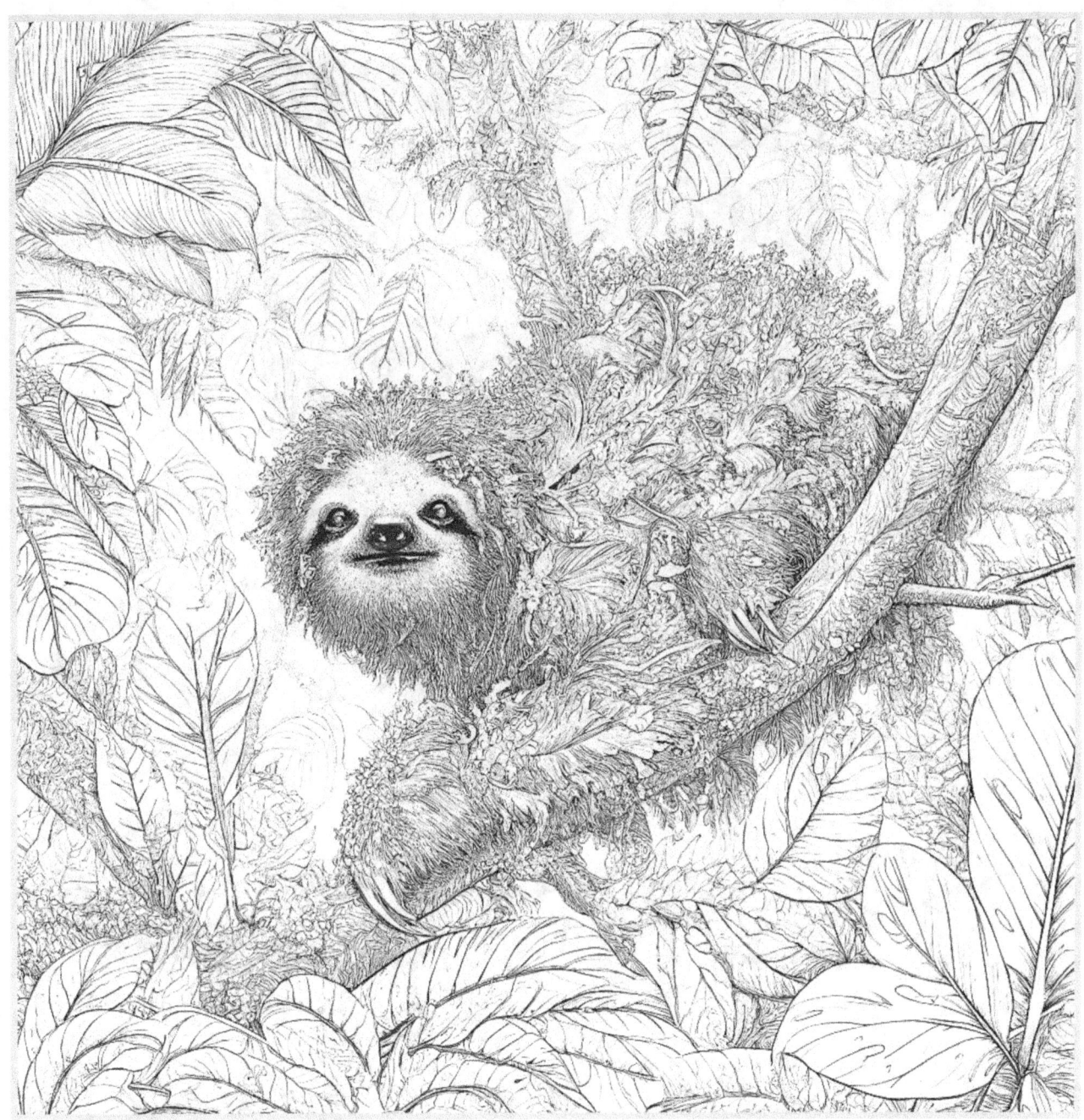

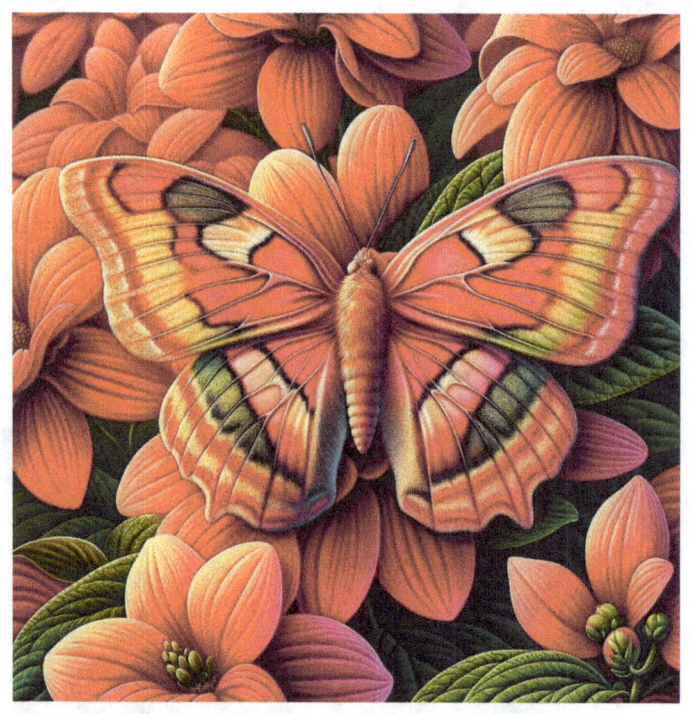

Jenifer Steller

Creative concepts developed in the organization and writing of this book are the creative and intellectual property of Jenifer J. Steller. All materials are commercially licensed.

www.ingramcontent.com/pod-product-compliance
Lightning Source LLC
Chambersburg PA
CBHW082358220526
45470CB00008B/2788